HUMAN ALL TOO HUMAN

A BOOK FOR FREE SPIRITS

BY
FRIEDRICH NIETZSCHE

TRANSLATED BY ALEXANDER HARVEY

Published and Distributed by:
Angelnook Publishing, Inc.
1277 Cranston Street
Cranston, RI 02920
www.angelnookpublishing.com

Copyright © 2012 Angelnook Publishing, Inc.
No part of this book may be reproduced in any form or by any electronic or mechanical means including information storage and retrieval systems without the express written consent of Angelnook Publishing, Inc.

All rights reserved.

ISBN: 1481189255
ISBN-13: 978-1481189255

ABOUT THE COVER ARTIST

Born and raised in Providence, RI, Paul Spremulli credits his traditional spiritual foundation to his parents, John and Pauline Spremulli. They instilled within him a unique blend of truth and confidence, combined with values of hard work, ethics, and fellowship.

Paul is an artist, writer, and spiritual healer and it was his passion for all three that became the seed that has been cultivated into the creation of Angelnook Publishing and The Angelnook Gallery and Spiritual Learning Center.

Through Angelnook, Paul hopes to share the art and the written word delivered to him by God. Paul's mission is to spread these messages of peace, beauty, inspiration, and spiritual fulfillment that have helped him throughout his life and made him the Renaissance man that he is today.

TABLE OF CONTENTS

PREFACE	1.
OF THE FIRST AND LAST THINGS	11.
HISTORY OF MORAL FEELINGS	43.
THE RELIGIOUS LIFE	89.

A NOTE FROM THE PUBLISHER

Angelnook Publishing takes great care when providing works previously published and / or written in a time that allowed for different spelling and grammatical rules to offer the most clear, concise, and accurate representation of the author's work.

As a result of such, some words in the following book may not necessarily follow traditional spelling and / or grammatical guidelines used in the mainstream industry today. However, the errors that exist within this manuscript have been left to better provide a more accurate representation of the intentions of the author. Changes have only been made when there would be no influence upon the wording or translation of the script.

Enjoy.

HUMAN ALL TOO HUMAN

A BOOK FOR FREE SPIRITS

BY
FRIEDRICH NIETZSCHE

TRANSLATED BY ALEXANDER HARVEY

PREFACE

1

It is often enough, and always with great surprise, intimated to me that there is something both ordinary and unusual in all my writings, from the "Birth of Tragedy" to the recently published "Prelude to a Philosophy of the Future": they all contain, I have been told, snares and nets for short sighted birds, and something that is almost a constant, subtle, incitement to an overturning of habitual opinions and of approved customs. What!? Everything is merely—human—all too human? With this exclamation my writings are gone through, not without a certain dread and mistrust of ethic itself and not without a disposition to ask the exponent of evil things if those things be not simply misrepresented. My writings have been termed a school of distrust, still more of disdain: also, and more happily, of courage, audacity even. And in fact, I myself do not believe that anybody ever looked into the world with a distrust as deep as mine, seeming, as I do, not simply the timely advocate of the devil, but, to employ theological terms, an enemy and challenger of God; and whosoever has experienced any of the consequences of such deep distrust, anything of the chills and the agonies of isolation to which such an unqualified difference of standpoint condemns him endowed with it, will also understand how often I must have sought relief and self-forgetfulness from any source—through any object of veneration or enmity, of scientific seriousness or wanton lightness; also why I, when I could not find what I was in need of, had to fashion it for myself, counterfeiting it or imagining it (and what poet or writer has ever done anything else, and what other purpose can all the art in the world possibly have?) That which I always stood most in need of in order to effect my cure and self-recovery was faith, faith enough not to be thus isolated, not to look at life from so singular a point of view—a magic apprehension (in eye and mind) of relationship and equality, a calm confidence in friendship, a blindness, free from suspicion and questioning, to two sidedness; a pleasure in externals, superficialities, the near, the accessible, in all things possessed of color, skin and seeming. Perhaps I could be fairly reproached with much "art" in this regard, many fine counterfeitings; for example, that, wisely or wilfully, I had shut my eyes to Schopenhauer's blind will towards ethic, at a time when I was already clear sighted enough on the subject of ethic; likewise that I had deceived myself concerning Richard Wagner's incurable romanticism, as if it were a beginning and not an end; likewise concerning the Greeks, likewise concerning the Germans and their future—and there may be, perhaps, a long list of such likewises. Granted, however, that all this were true, and with justice urged against me, what does it signify, what can it signify in regard to how much of the self-sustaining capacity, how much of reason and higher protection are embraced in such self-deception?—and how much more falsity is still necessary to me that I may therewith always reassure myself regarding the luxury of my truth. Enough, I still live; and life is not considered now apart from ethic; it *will* [have] deception; it thrives (lebt) on deception ... but am I not beginning to do all over again what I have always done, I, the old immoralist, and bird snarer—talk unmorally, ultramorally, "beyond good and evil"?

2

Thus, then, have I evolved for myself the "free spirits" to

whom this discouraging-encouraging work, under the general title "Human, All Too Human," is dedicated. Such "free spirits" do not really exist and never did exist. But I stood in need of them, as I have pointed out, in order that some good might be mixed with my evils (illness, loneliness, strangeness, *acedia*, incapacity): to serve as gay spirits and comrades, with whom one may talk and laugh when one is disposed to talk and laugh, and whom one may send to the devil when they grow wearisome. They are some compensation for the lack of friends. That such free spirits can possibly exist, that our Europe will yet number among her sons of to-morrow or of the day after to-morrow, such a brilliant and enthusiastic company, alive and palpable and not merely, as in my case, fantasms and imaginary shades, I, myself, can by no means doubt. I see them already coming, slowly, slowly. May it not be that I am doing a little something to expedite their coming when I describe in advance the influences under which I see them evolving and the ways along which they travel?

3

It may be conjectured that a soul in which the type of "free spirit" can attain maturity and completeness had its decisive and deciding event in the form of a great emancipation or unbinding, and that prior to that event it seemed only the more firmly and forever chained to its place and pillar. What binds strongest? What cords seem almost unbreakable? In the case of mortals of a choice and lofty nature they will be those of duty: that reverence, which in youth is most typical, that timidity and tenderness in the presence of the traditionally honored and the worthy, that gratitude to the soil from which we sprung, for the hand that guided us, for the relic before which we were taught to pray—their sublimest moments will themselves bind these souls most strongly. The great liberation comes suddenly to such prisoners, like an earthquake: the young soul is all at once shaken, torn apart, cast forth—it comprehends not itself what is taking place. An involuntary onward impulse rules them with the mastery of command; a will, a wish are developed to go forward, anywhere, at any price; a strong, dangerous curiosity regarding an undiscovered world flames and flashes in all their being. "Better to die than live *here*"—so sounds the tempting voice: and this "here," this "at home" constitutes all they have hitherto loved. A sudden dread and distrust of that which they loved, a flash of contempt for that which is called their "duty," a mutinous, wilful, volcanic-like longing for a far away journey, strange scenes and people, annihilation, petrifaction, a hatred surmounting love, perhaps a sacrilegious impulse and look backwards, to where they so long prayed and loved, perhaps a flush of shame for what they did and at the same time an exultation at having done it, an inner, intoxicating, delightful tremor in which is betrayed the sense of victory—a victory? over what? over whom? a riddle-like victory, fruitful in questioning and well worth questioning, but the *first* victory, for all—such things of pain and ill belong to the history of the great liberation. And it is at the same time a malady that can destroy a man, this first outbreak of strength and will for self-destination, self-valuation, this will for free will: and how much illness is forced to the surface in the frantic strivings and singularities with which the freedman, the liberated seeks henceforth to attest his mastery over things! He roves fiercely around, with an unsatisfied longing and whatever objects he may encounter must suffer from the perilous expectancy of his pride; he tears to pieces whatever attracts him. With a sardonic laugh he overturns whatever he finds veiled or protected by any reverential awe: he would see what these things look like when they are overturned. It is wilfulness and delight in the wilfulness of it, if he now, perhaps, gives his approval to that which has heretofore been in ill repute—if, in curiosity and experiment, he penetrates stealthily to the most forbidden things. In the background during all his plunging and roaming—for he is as restless and aimless in his course as if lost in a wilderness—is the interrogation mark of a curiosity growing ever more dangerous. "Can we not upset every standard? and is good perhaps evil? and God only an invention and a subtlety of the devil? Is everything, in the last resort, false? And if we are dupes are we not on that very account dupers also? *must* we not be dupers also?" Such reflections lead and mislead him, ever further on, ever further away. Solitude, that dread goddess and mater saeva cupidinum, encircles and besets him, ever more threatening, more violent, more heart breaking—but who to-day knows what solitude is?

4

From this morbid solitude, from the deserts of such trial years, the way is yet far to that great, overflowing certainty and healthiness which cannot dispense even with sickness as a means and a grappling hook of knowledge; to that matured freedom of the spirit which is, in an equal degree, self mastery and discipline of the heart, and gives access to the path of much and various reflection—to that inner comprehensiveness and self satisfaction of over-richness which precludes all danger that the spirit has gone astray even in its own path and is sitting intoxicated in some corner or other; to that overplus of plastic, healing, imitative and restorative power which is the very sign of vigorous health, that overplus which confers upon the free spirit the perilous prerogative of spending a life in experiment and of running adventurous risks: the past-master-privilege of the free spirit. In the interval there may be long years of convalescence, years filled with many hued painfully-bewitching transformations, dominated and led to the goal by a tenacious will for health that is often emboldened to assume the guise and the disguise of health. There is a middle ground to this, which a man of such destiny can not subsequently recall without emotion; he basks in a special fine sun of his own, with a feeling of birdlike freedom, birdlike visual power, birdlike irrepressibleness, a something extraneous (Drittes) in which curiosity and delicate disdain have united. A "free spirit"—this refreshing term is grateful in any mood, it almost sets one aglow. One lives—no longer in the bonds of love and hate, without a yes or no, here or there indifferently, best pleased to evade, to avoid, to beat about, neither advancing nor retreating. One is habituated to the bad, like a person who all at once sees a fearful hurly-burly *beneath* him—and one was the counterpart of him who bothers himself with things that do not concern him. As a matter of fact the free spirit is bothered with mere things—and how many things—which no longer *concern* him.

5

A step further in recovery: and the free spirit draws near to life again, slowly indeed, almost refractorily, almost distrustfully. There is again warmth and mellowness: feeling and fellow feeling acquire depth, lambent airs stir all about him. He almost feels: it seems as if now for the first time his eyes are open to things *near*. He is in amaze and sits hushed: for where had he been? These near and immediate things: how changed they seem to him! He looks gratefully back—grateful for his wandering, his self exile and severity, his lookings afar and his bird flights in the cold heights. How fortunate that he has not, like a sensitive, dull home body, remained always "in the house" and "at home!" He had been beside himself, beyond a doubt. Now for the first time he really sees himself—and what surprises in the process. What hitherto unfelt tremors! Yet what joy in the exhaustion, the old sickness, the relapses of the convalescent! How it delights him, suffering, to sit still, to exercise patience, to lie in the sun! Who so well as he appreciates the fact that there comes balmy weather even in winter, who delights more in the sunshine athwart the wall? They are the most appreciative creatures in the world, and also the most humble, these convalescents and lizards, crawling back towards life: there are some among them who can let no day slip past them without addressing some song of praise to its retreating light. And speaking seriously, it is a fundamental cure for all pessimism (the cankerous vice, as is well known, of all idealists and humbugs), to become ill in the manner of these free spirits, to remain ill quite a while and then bit by bit grow healthy—I mean healthier. It is wisdom, worldly wisdom, to administer even health to oneself for a long time in small doses.

6

About this time it becomes at last possible, amid the flash lights of a still unestablished, still precarious health, for the free, the ever freer spirit to begin to read the riddle of that great liberation, a riddle which has hitherto lingered, obscure, well worth questioning, almost impalpable, in his memory. If once he hardly dared to ask "why so apart? so alone? renouncing all I loved? renouncing respect itself? why this coldness, this suspicion, this hate for one's very virtues?" —now he dares, and asks it loudly, already hearing the answer, "you had to become master over yourself, master of your own good qualities. Formerly they were your masters: but they should be merely your tools along with other tools. You had to acquire power over your aye and no and learn to hold and withhold them in accordance with your higher aims. You had to grasp the perspective of every representation (Werthschätzung)—the dislocation, distortion and the apparent end or teleology of the horizon, besides whatever else appertains to the perspective: also the element of demerit in its relation to opposing merit, and the whole intellectual cost of every affirmative, every negative. You had to find out the *inevitable* error* in every Yes and in every No, error as inseparable from life, life itself as conditioned by the perspective and its inaccuracy.* Above all, you had to see with your own eyes where the error* is always greatest: there, namely, where life is littlest, narrowest, meanest, least developed and yet cannot help looking upon itself as the goal and standard of things, and smugly and ignobly and incessantly tearing to tatters all that is highest and greatest and richest, and putting the shreds into the form of questions from the standpoint of its own well being. You had to see with your own eyes the problem of classification, (Rangordnung, regulation concerning rank and station) and how strength and sweep and reach of perspective wax upward together: You had"—enough, the free spirit knows henceforward which "you had" it has obeyed and also what it now can do and

---

* Ungerechtigkeit, literally wrongfulness, injustice, unrighteousness.

what it now, for the first time, *dare*.

7

Accordingly, the free spirit works out for itself an answer to that riddle of its liberation and concludes by generalizing upon its experience in the following fashion: "What I went through everyone must go through" in whom any problem is germinated and strives to body itself forth. The inner power and inevitability of this problem will assert themselves in due course, as in the case of any unsuspected pregnancy—long before the spirit has seen this problem in its true aspect and learned to call it by its right name. Our destiny exercises its influence over us even when, as yet, we have not learned its nature: it is our future that lays down the law to our to-day. Granted, that it is the problem of classification* of which we free spirits may say, this is *our* problem, yet it is only now, in the midday of our life, that we fully appreciate what preparations, shifts, trials, ordeals, stages, were essential to that problem before it could emerge to our view, and why we had to go through the various and contradictory longings and satisfactions of body and soul, as circumnavigators and adventurers of that inner world called "man"; as surveyors of that "higher" and of that "progression"† that is also called "man"—crowding in everywhere, almost without fear, disdaining nothing, missing nothing, testing everything, sifting everything and eliminating the chance impurities—until at last we could say, we free spirits: "Here—a *new* problem! Here, a long ladder on the rungs of which we ourselves have rested and risen, which we have actually been at times. Here is a something higher, a something deeper, a something below us, a vastly extensive order, (Ordnung) a comparative classification (Rangordnung), that we perceive: here—*our* problem!"

---

* Rangordnung: the meaning is "the problem of grasping the relative importance of things."
† Uebereinander: one over another.

FRIEDRICH NIETZSCHE

8

To what stage in the development just outlined the present book belongs (or is assigned) is something that will be hidden from no augur or psychologist for an instant. But where are there psychologists to-day? In France, certainly; in Russia, perhaps; certainly not in Germany. Grounds are not wanting, to be sure, upon which the Germans of to-day may adduce this fact to their credit: unhappily for one who in this matter is fashioned and mentored in an un-German school! This *German* book, which has found its readers in a wide circle of lands and peoples—it has been some ten years on its rounds—and which must make its way by means of any musical art and tune that will captivate the foreign ear as well as the native—this book has been read most indifferently in Germany itself and little heeded there: to what is that due? "It requires too much," I have been told, "it addresses itself to men free from the press of petty obligations, it demands fine and trained perceptions, it requires a surplus, a surplus of time, of the lightness of heaven and of the heart, of otium in the most unrestricted sense: mere good things that we Germans of to-day have not got and therefore cannot give." After so graceful a retort, my philosophy bids me be silent and ask no more questions: at times, as the proverb says, one remains a philosopher only because one says—nothing!

Nice, Spring, 1886.

OF THE FIRST AND LAST THINGS

1
Chemistry of the Notions and the Feelings

Philosophical problems, in almost all their aspects, present themselves in the same interrogative formula now that they did two thousand years ago: how can a thing develop out of its antithesis? for example, the reasonable from the non-reasonable, the animate from the inanimate, the logical from the illogical, altruism from egoism, disinterestedness from greed, truth from error? The metaphysical philosophy formerly steered itself clear of this difficulty to such extent as to repudiate the evolution of one thing from another and to assign a miraculous origin to what it deemed highest and best, due to the very nature and being of the "thing-in-itself." The historical philosophy, on the other hand, which can no longer be viewed apart from physical science, the youngest of all philosophical methods, discovered experimentally (and its results will probably always be the same) that there is no antithesis whatever, except in the usual exaggerations of popular or metaphysical comprehension, and that an error of the reason is at the bottom of such contradiction. According to its explanation, there is, strictly speaking, neither unselfish conduct, nor a wholly disinterested point of view. Both are simply sublimations in which the basic element seems almost evaporated and betrays its presence only to the keenest observation. All that we need and that could possibly be given us in the present state of development of the sciences, is a chemistry of the moral, religious, aesthetic conceptions and feeling, as well as of those emotions which we experience in the affairs, great and small, of society and civilization, and which we are sensible of even in solitude. But what if this chemistry established the fact that, even in *its* domain, the most magnificent results were attained with the basest and most despised ingredients? Would many feel disposed to continue such investigations? Mankind loves to put by the questions of its origin and beginning: must one not be almost inhuman in order to follow the opposite course?

2
The Traditional Error of Philosophers

All philosophers make the common mistake of taking contemporary man as their starting point and of trying, through an analysis of him, to reach a conclusion. "Man" involuntarily presents himself to them as an aeterna veritas as a passive element in every hurly-burly, as a fixed standard of things. Yet everything uttered by the philosopher on the subject of man is, in the last resort, nothing more than a piece of testimony concerning man during a very limited period of time. Lack of the historical sense is the traditional defect in all philosophers. Many innocently take man in his most childish state as fashioned through the influence of certain religious and even of certain political developments, as the permanent form under which man must be viewed. They will not learn that man has evolved,[*] that the intellectual faculty itself is an evolution, whereas some philosophers make the whole cosmos out of this intellectual faculty. But everything essential in human evolution took place aeons ago, long before the four thousand years or so of which we know anything: during these man may not have changed very

---

[*] geworden.

much. However, the philosopher ascribes "instinct" to contemporary man and assumes that this is one of the unalterable facts regarding man himself, and hence affords a clue to the understanding of the universe in general. The whole teleology is so planned that man during the last four thousand years shall be spoken of as a being existing from all eternity, and with reference to whom everything in the cosmos from its very inception is naturally ordered. Yet everything evolved: there are no eternal facts as there are no absolute truths. Accordingly, historical philosophising is henceforth indispensable, and with it honesty of judgment.

3
Appreciation of Simple Truths

It is the characteristic of an advanced civilization to set a higher value upon little, simple truths, ascertained by scientific method, than upon the pleasing and magnificent errors originating in metaphysical and æsthetical epochs and peoples. To begin with, the former are spoken of with contempt as if there could be no question of comparison respecting them, so rigid, homely, prosaic and even discouraging is the aspect of the first, while so beautiful, decorative, intoxicating and perhaps beatific appear the last named. Nevertheless, the hardwon, the certain, the lasting and, therefore, the fertile in new knowledge, is the higher; to hold fast to it is manly and evinces courage, directness, endurance. And not only individual men but all mankind will by degrees be uplifted to this manliness when they are finally habituated to the proper appreciation of tenable, enduring knowledge and have lost all faith in inspiration and in the miraculous revelation of truth. The reverers of forms, indeed, with their standards of beauty and taste, may have good reason to laugh when the appreciation of little truths and the scientific spirit begin to prevail, but that will be only because their eyes are not yet opened to the charm of the utmost simplicity of form or because men though reared in the rightly appreciative spirit, will still not be fully permeated by it, so that they continue unwittingly imitating ancient forms (and that ill enough, as anybody does who no longer feels any interest in a thing). Formerly the mind was not brought into play through the medium of exact thought. Its serious business lay in the working out of forms and symbols. That has now changed. Any seriousness in symbolism is at present the indication of a deficient education. As our very acts become more intellectual, our tendencies more rational, and our judgment, for example, as to what seems reasonable, is very different from what it was a hundred years ago: so the forms of our lives grow ever more intellectual and, to the old fashioned eye, perhaps, uglier, but only because it cannot see that the richness of inner, rational beauty always spreads and deepens, and that the inner, rational aspect of all things should now be of more consequence to us than the most beautiful externality and the most exquisite limning.

4
Astrology and the Like

It is presumable that the objects of the religious, moral, aesthetic and logical notions pertain simply to the superficialities of things, although man flatters himself with the thought that here at least he is getting to the heart of the cosmos. He deceives himself because these things have power to make him so happy and so wretched, and so he evinces, in this respect, the same conceit that characterises astrology. Astrology presupposes that the heavenly bodies are regulated in their movements in harmony with the destiny of mortals: the moral man presupposes that that which concerns himself most nearly must also be the heart and soul of things.

5
Misconception of Dreams

In the dream, mankind, in epochs of crude primitive civilization, thought they were introduced to a second, substantial world: here we have the source of all metaphysic. Without the dream, men would never have been incited to an analysis of the world. Even the distinction between soul and body is wholly due to the primitive conception of the dream, as also the hypothesis of the embodied soul, whence the development of all superstition, and also, probably, the belief in god. "The dead still live: for they appear to the living in dreams." So reasoned mankind at one time, and through many thousands of years.

6
The Scientific Spirit Prevails only Partially, not Wholly

The specialized, minutest departments of science are dealt with purely objectively. But the general universal sciences, considered as a great, basic unity, posit the question—truly a very living question—: to what purpose? what is the use? Because of this reference to utility they are, as a whole, less impersonal than when looked at in their specialized aspects. Now in the case of philosophy, as forming the apex of the scientific pyramid, this question of the utility of knowledge is necessarily brought very conspicuously forward, so that every philosophy has, unconsciously, the air of ascribing the highest utility to itself. It is for this reason that all philosophies contain such a great amount of high flying metaphysic, and such a shrinking from the seeming insignificance of the deliverances of physical science: for the significance of knowledge in relation to life must be made to appear as great as possible. This constitutes the antagonism between the specialties of science and philosophy. The latter aims, as art aims, at imparting to life and conduct the utmost depth and significance: in the former mere knowledge is sought and nothing else—whatever else be incidentally obtained. Heretofore there has never been a philosophical system in which philosophy itself was not made the apologist of knowledge [in the abstract]. On this point, at least, each is optimistic and insists that to knowledge the highest utility must be ascribed. They are all under the tyranny of logic, which is, from its very nature, optimism.

7
The Discordant Element in Science

Philosophy severed itself from science when it put the question: what is that knowledge of the world and of life through which mankind may be made happiest? This happened when the Socratic school arose: with the standpoint of *happiness* the arteries of investigating science were compressed too tightly to permit of any circulation of the blood—and are so compressed to-day.

8
Pneumatic Explanation of Nature[*]

Metaphysic reads the message of nature as if it were written purely pneumatically, as the church and its learned ones formerly did where the bible was concerned. It requires a great deal of expertness to apply to nature the same strict science of interpretation that the philologists have devised for all literature, and to apply it for the purpose of a simple, direct interpretation of the message, and at the same time, not bring out a double meaning. But, as in the case of books and literature, errors of exposition are far from being completely eliminated, and vestiges of allegorical and mystical interpretations are still to be met with in the most cultivated circles, so where nature is concerned the case is—actually much worse.

9
Metaphysical World

It is true, there may be a metaphysical world; the absolute possibility of it can scarcely be disputed. We see all things through the medium of the human head and we cannot well cut

---

[*] Pneumatic is here used in the sense of spiritual. Pneuma being the Greek word in the New Testament for the Holy Spirit.—Ed.

off this head: although there remains the question what part of the world would be left after it had been cut off. But that is a purely abstract scientific problem and one not much calculated to give men uneasiness: yet everything that has heretofore made metaphysical assumptions valuable, fearful or delightful to men, all that gave rise to them is passion, error and self deception: the worst systems of knowledge, not the best, pin their tenets of belief thereto. When such methods are once brought to view as the basis of all existing religions and metaphysics, they are already discredited. There always remains, however, the possibility already conceded: but nothing at all can be made out of that, to say not a word about letting happiness, salvation and life hang upon the threads spun from such a possibility. Accordingly, nothing could be predicated of the metaphysical world beyond the fact that it is an elsewhere,* another sphere, inaccessible and incomprehensible to us: it would become a thing of negative properties. Even were the existence of such a world absolutely established, it would nevertheless remain incontrovertible that of all kinds of knowledge, knowledge of such a world would be of least consequence—of even less consequence than knowledge of the chemical analysis of water would be to a storm tossed mariner.

10
The Harmlessness of Metaphysic in the Future

As soon as religion, art and ethics are so understood that a full comprehension of them can be gained without taking refuge in the postulates of metaphysical claptrap at any point in the line of reasoning, there will be a complete cessation of interest in the purely theoretical problem of the "thing in itself" and the "phenomenon." For here, too, the same truth applies: in religion, art and ethics we are not concerned with the "essence of the cosmos".† We are in the sphere of pure conception. No

---
* Anderssein
† "Wesen der Welt an sich."

presentiment [or intuition] can carry us any further. With perfect tranquility the question of how our conception of the world could differ so sharply from the actual world as it is manifest to us, will be relegated to the physiological sciences and to the history of the evolution of ideas and organisms.

11
Language as a Presumptive Science

The importance of language in the development of civilization consists in the fact that by means of it man placed one world, his own, alongside another, a place of leverage that he thought so firm as to admit of his turning the rest of the cosmos on a pivot that he might master it. In so far as man for ages looked upon mere ideas and names of things as upon aeternae veritates, he evinced the very pride with which he raised himself above the brute. He really supposed that in language he possessed a knowledge of the cosmos. The language builder was not so modest as to believe that he was only giving names to things. On the contrary he thought he embodied the highest wisdom concerning things in [mere] words; and, in truth, language is the first movement in all strivings for wisdom. Here, too, it is *faith in ascertained truth*[*] from which the mightiest fountains of strength have flowed. Very tardily—only now—it dawns upon men that they have propagated a monstrous error in their belief in language. Fortunately, it is too late now to arrest and turn back the evolutionary process of the reason, which had its inception in this belief. Logic itself rests upon assumptions to which nothing in the world of reality corresponds. For example, the correspondence of certain things to one another and the identity of those things at different periods of time are assumptions pure and simple, but the science of logic originated in the positive belief that they were not assumptions at all but established facts. It is the same with the science of mathematics

---

[*] Glaube an die gefundene Wahrheit, as distinguished from faith in what is taken on trust as truth.

which certainly would never have come into existence if mankind had known from the beginning that in all nature there is no perfectly straight line, no true circle, no standard of measurement.

12
Dream and Civilization

The function of the brain which is most encroached upon in slumber is the memory; not that it is wholly suspended, but it is reduced to a state of imperfection as, in primitive ages of mankind, was probably the case with everyone, whether waking or sleeping. Uncontrolled and entangled as it is, it perpetually confuses things as a result of the most trifling similarities, yet in the same mental confusion and lack of control the nations invented their mythologies, while nowadays travelers habitually observe how prone the savage is to forgetfulness, how his mind, after the least exertion of memory, begins to wander and lose itself until finally he utters falsehood and nonsense from sheer exhaustion. Yet, in dreams, we all resemble this savage. Inadequacy of distinction and error of comparison are the basis of the preposterous things we do and say in dreams, so that when we clearly recall a dream we are startled that so much idiocy lurks within us. The absolute distinctness of all dream-images, due to implicit faith in their substantial reality, recalls the conditions in which earlier mankind were placed, for whom hallucinations had extraordinary vividness, entire communities and even entire nations laboring simultaneously under them. Therefore: in sleep and in dream we make the pilgrimage of early mankind over again.

13
Logic of the Dream

During sleep the nervous system, through various inner provocatives, is in constant agitation. Almost all the organs act independently and vigorously. The blood circulates rapidly. The posture of the sleeper compresses some portions of the body. The coverlets influence the sensations in different ways. The stomach carries on the digestive process and acts upon other organs thereby. The intestines are in motion. The position of the head induces unaccustomed action. The feet, shoeless, no longer pressing the ground, are the occasion of other sensations of novelty, as is, indeed, the changed garb of the entire body. All these things, following the bustle and change of the day, result, through their novelty, in a movement throughout the entire system that extends even to the brain functions. Thus there are a hundred circumstances to induce perplexity in the mind, a questioning as to the cause of this excitation. Now, the dream is a *seeking and presenting of reasons* for these excitations of feeling, of the supposed reasons, that is to say. Thus, for example, whoever has his feet bound with two threads will probably dream that a pair of serpents are coiled about his feet. This is at first a hypothesis, then a belief with an accompanying imaginative picture and the argument: "these snakes must be the *causa* of those sensations which I, the sleeper, now have." So reasons the mind of the sleeper. The conditions precedent, as thus conjectured, become, owing to the excitation of the fancy, present realities. Everyone knows from experience how a dreamer will transform one piercing sound, for example, that of a bell, into another of quite a different nature, say, the report of cannon. In his dream he becomes aware first of the effects, which he explains by a subsequent hypothesis and becomes persuaded of the purely conjectural nature of the sound. But how comes it that the mind of the dreamer goes so far astray when the same mind, awake, is habitually cautious, careful, and so conservative in its dealings with hypotheses? Why does the first plausible hypothesis of the cause of a sensation gain credit in the dreaming state? (For in a dream we look upon that dream as reality, that is, we accept our hypotheses as fully established). I have no doubt that as men argue in their dreams to-day, mankind argued, even in their waking moments, for thousands of years: the first *causa*, that occurred to the mind with reference to anything that stood in need of explanation, was accepted as the true explanation and served as such. (Savages show the same tendency in operation, as the reports of travelers agree). In the dream this atavistic relic of humanity manifests its existence within us, for it is the foundation upon which the higher rational faculty developed itself and still develops itself in every individual. Dreams carry us back to the earlier stages of human culture and afford us a means of understanding it more clearly. Dream thought comes so easily to us now because we are so thoroughly trained to it through the interminable stages of evolution during which this fanciful and facile form of theorising has prevailed. To a certain extent the dream is a restorative for the brain, which, during the day, is called upon to meet the many demands for trained thought made upon it by the conditions of a higher civilization.—We may, if we please, become sensible, even in our waking moments, of a condition that is as a door and vestibule to dreaming. If we close our eyes the brain immediately conjures up a medley of impressions of light and color, apparently a sort of imitation and echo of the impressions forced in upon the brain during its waking moments. And now the mind, in co-operation with the imagination, transforms this formless play of light and color into definite figures, moving groups, landscapes. What really takes place is a sort of reasoning from effect back to cause. As the brain inquires: whence these impressions of light and color? it posits as the inducing causes of such lights and colors, those shapes and figures. They serve the brain as the occasions of those lights and colors because the brain, when the eyes are open and the senses awake, is accustomed to perceiving the cause of every impression of light and color made upon it. Here again the imagination is continually interposing its images inasmuch as it participates in the production of the impressions made through the senses day by day; and the dream-fancy does exactly the same thing—that is, the presumed cause is determined from the effect and *after* the effect: all this, too, with extraordinary rapidity, so that in this matter, as in a matter of jugglery or sleight-of-hand, a confusion of the mind is produced and an after effect is made to appear a simultaneous action, an inverted succession of events, even. —

From these considerations we can see how *late* strict, logical thought, the true notion of cause and effect must have been in developing, since our intellectual and rational faculties to this very day revert to these primitive processes of deduction, while practically half our lifetime is spent in the super-inducing conditions.—Even the poet, the artist, ascribes to his sentimental and emotional states causes which are not the true ones. To that extent he is a reminder of early mankind and can aid us in its comprehension.

14
Association[*]

All strong feelings are associated with a variety of allied sentiments and emotions. They stir up the memory at the same time. When we are under their influence we are reminded of similar states and we feel a renewal of them within us. Thus are formed habitual successions of feelings and notions, which, at last, when they follow one another with lightning rapidity are no longer felt as complexities but as unities. In this sense we hear of moral feelings, of religious feelings, as if they were absolute unities. In reality they are streams with a hundred sources and tributaries. Here again, the unity of the word speaks nothing for the unity of the thing.

15
No Within and Without in the World[†]

As Democritus transferred the notions above and below to limitless space, where they are destitute of meaning, so the philosophers do generally with the idea "within and without," as regards the form and substance (Wesen und Erscheinung) of the

---

[*] Miterklingen: to sound simultaneously with.

[†] Kein Innen und Aussen in der Welt: the above translation may seem too literal but some dispute has arisen concerning the precise idea the author means to convey.

world. What they claim is that through the medium of profound feelings one can penetrate deep into the soul of things (Innre), draw close to the heart of nature. But these feelings are deep only in so far as with them are simultaneously aroused, although almost imperceptibly, certain complicated groups of thoughts (Gedankengruppen) which we call deep: a feeling is deep because we deem the thoughts accompanying it deep. But deep thought can nevertheless be very widely sundered from truth, as for instance every metaphysical thought. Take from deep feeling the element of thought blended with it and all that remains is *strength* of feeling which is no voucher for the validity of knowledge, as intense faith is evidence only of its own intensity and not of the truth of that in which the faith is felt.

16
Phenomenon and Thing-in-Itself

The philosophers are in the habit of placing themselves in front of life and experience—that which they call the world of phenomena—as if they were standing before a picture that is unrolled before them in its final completeness. This panorama, they think, must be studied in every detail in order to reach some conclusion regarding the object represented by the picture. From effect, accordingly is deduced cause and from cause is deduced the unconditioned. This process is generally looked upon as affording the all sufficient explanation of the world of phenomena. On the other hand one must, (while putting the conception of the metaphysical distinctly forward as that of the unconditioned, and consequently of the unconditioning) absolutely deny any connection between the unconditioned (of the metaphysical world) and the world known to us: so that throughout phenomena there is no manifestation of the thing-in-itself, and getting from one to the other is out of the question. Thus is left quite ignored the circumstance that the picture—that which we now call life and experience—is a gradual evolution, is, indeed, still in process of evolution and for that reason should not be regarded as an enduring whole from which any conclusion as to its author (the all-sufficient reason) could be arrived at, or even pronounced out of the question. It is because we have for thousands of years looked into the world with moral, aesthetic, religious predispositions, with blind prejudice, passion or fear, and surfeited ourselves with indulgence in the follies of illogical thought, that the world has gradually become so wondrously motley, frightful, significant, soulful: it has taken on tints, but we have been the colorists: the human intellect, upon the foundation of human needs, of human passions, has reared all these "phenomena" and injected its own erroneous fundamental conceptions into things. Late, very late, the human intellect checks itself: and now the world of experience and the thing-in-itself seem to it so severed and so antithetical that it denies the possibility of one's hinging upon the other—or else summons us to surrender our intellect, our personal will, to the secret and the awe-inspiring in order that thereby we may attain certainty of certainty hereafter. Again, there are those who have combined all the characteristic features of our world of phenomena—that is, the conception of the world which has been formed and inherited through a series of intellectual vagaries—and instead of holding the intellect responsible for it all, have pronounced the very nature of things accountable for the present very sinister aspect of the world, and preached annihilation of existence. Through all these views and opinions the toilsome, steady process of science (which now for the first time begins to celebrate its greatest triumph in the genesis of thought) will definitely work itself out, the result, being, perhaps, to the following effect: That which we now call the world is the result of a crowd of errors and fancies which gradually developed in the general evolution of organic nature, have grown together and been transmitted to us as the accumulated treasure of all the past—as the *treasure*, for whatever is worth anything in our humanity rests upon it. From this world of conception it is in the power of science to release us only to a slight extent—and this is all that could be wished—inasmuch as it cannot eradicate the influence of hereditary habits of feeling, but it can light up by degrees the stages of the development of that world of conception, and lift us, at least for a time, above the whole spectacle. Perhaps we may then perceive that the thing-in-itself is a meet subject for Homeric laughter: that it seemed so much, everything, indeed, and is really a void—void, that is to say, of meaning.

17
Metaphysical Explanation

Man, when he is young, prizes metaphysical explanations, because they make him see matters of the highest import in things he found disagreeable or contemptible: and if he is not satisfied with himself, this feeling of dissatisfaction is soothed when he sees the most hidden world-problem or world-pain in that which he finds so displeasing in himself. To feel himself more unresponsible and at the same time to find things (Dinge) more interesting—that is to him the double benefit he owes to metaphysics. Later, indeed, he acquires distrust of the whole metaphysical method of explaining things: he then perceives, perhaps, that those effects could have been attained just as well and more scientifically by another method: that physical and historical explanations would, at least, have given that feeling of freedom from personal responsibility just as well, while interest in life and its problems would be stimulated, perhaps, even more.

18
The Fundamental Problems of Metaphysics

If a history of the development of thought is ever written, the following proposition, advanced by a distinguished logician, will be illuminated with a new light: "The universal, primordial law of the apprehending subject consists in the inner necessity of cognizing every object by itself, as in its essence a thing unto itself, therefore as self-existing and unchanging, in short, as a substance." Even this law, which is here called "primordial," is an evolution: it has yet to be shown how gradually this evolution takes place in lower organizations: how the dim, mole eyes of such organizations see, at first, nothing but a blank sameness: how later, when the various excitations of desire and aversion manifest themselves, various substances are gradually distinguished, but each with an attribute, that is, a special relationship to such an organization. The first step towards the logical is judgment, the essence of which, according to the best logicians, is belief. At the foundation of all beliefs lie sensations of pleasure or pain in relation to the apprehending subject. A third feeling, as the result of two prior, single, separate feelings, is judgment in its crudest form. We organic beings are primordially interested by nothing whatever in any thing (Ding) except its relation to ourselves with reference to pleasure and pain. Between the moments in which we are conscious of this relation, (the states of feeling) lie the moments of rest, of not-feeling: then the world and every thing (Ding) have no interest for us: we observe no change in them (as at present a person absorbed in something does not notice anyone passing by). To plants all things are, as a rule, at rest, eternal, every object like itself. From the period of lower organisms has been handed down to man the belief that there are like things (gleiche Dinge): only the trained experience attained through the most advanced science contradicts this postulate. The primordial belief of all organisms is, perhaps, that all the rest of the world is one thing and motionless.—Furthest away from this first step towards the logical is the notion of causation: even to-day we think that all our feelings and doings are, at bottom, acts of the free will; when the sentient individual contemplates himself he deems every feeling, every change, a something isolated, disconnected, that is to say, unqualified by any thing; it comes suddenly to the surface, independent of anything that went before or came after. We are hungry, but originally we do not know that the organism must be nourished: on the contrary that feeling seems to manifest itself without reason or purpose; it stands out by itself and seems quite independent. Therefore: the belief in the freedom of the will is a primordial error of everything organic as old as the very earliest inward prompting of the logical faculty; belief in unconditioned substances and in like things (gleiche Dinge) is also a primordial and equally ancient error of everything organic. Inasmuch as all metaphysic has concerned itself particularly with substance and with freedom of the will, it should be designated as the science that deals with the fundamental errors of mankind as if they were fundamental truths.

19
Number

The invention of the laws of number has as its basis the primordial and prior-prevailing delusion that many like things exist (although in point of fact there is no such thing is a duplicate), or that, at least, there are things (but there is no "thing"). The assumption of plurality always presupposes that *something* exists which manifests itself repeatedly, but just here is where the delusion prevails; in this very matter we feign realities, unities, that have no existence. Our feelings, notions, of space and time are false for they lead, when duly tested, to logical contradictions. In all scientific demonstrations we always unavoidably base our calculation upon some false standards [of duration or measurement] but as these standards are at least *constant*, as, for example, our notions of time and space, the results arrived at by science possess absolute accuracy and certainty in their relationship to one another: one can keep on building upon them—until is reached that final limit at which the erroneous fundamental conceptions, (the invariable breakdown) come into conflict with the results established—as, for example, in the case of the atomic theory. Here we always find ourselves obliged to give credence to a "thing" or material "substratum" that is set in motion, although, at the same time, the whole scientific programme has had as its aim the resolving of everything material into motions [themselves]: here again we distinguish with our feeling [that which does the] moving and [that which is] moved,* and we never get out of this circle,

---

* Wir scheiden auch hier noch mit unserer Empfindung Bewegendes und Bewegtes.

because the belief in things* has been from time immemorial rooted in our nature.—When Kant says "the intellect does not derive its laws from nature, but dictates them to her" he states the full truth as regards the *idea of nature* which we form (nature = world, as notion, that is, as error) but which is merely the synthesis of a host of errors of the intellect.

To a world not [the outcome of] our conception, the laws of number are wholly inapplicable: such laws are valid only in the world of mankind.

20
Some Backward Steps

One very forward step in education is taken when man emerges from his superstitious and religious ideas and fears and, for instance, no longer believes in the dear little angels or in original sin, and has stopped talking about the salvation of the soul: when he has taken this step to freedom he has, nevertheless, through the utmost exertion of his mental power, to overcome metaphysics. Then a backward movement is necessary: he must appreciate the historical justification, and to an equal extent the psychological considerations, in such a movement. He must understand that the greatest advances made by mankind have resulted from such a course and that without this very backward movement the highest achievements of man hitherto would have been impossible.—With regard to philosophical metaphysics I see ever more and more who have arrived at the negative goal (that all positive metaphysic is a delusion) but as yet very few who go a few steps backward: one should look out over the last rungs of the ladder, but not try to stand on them, that is to say. The most advanced as yet go only far enough to free themselves from metaphysic and look back at it with an air of superiority: whereas here, no less than in the hippodrome, it is necessary to turn around in order to reach the end of the course.

---

* Glaube an Dinge.

FRIEDRICH NIETZSCHE

21
Presumable [Nature of the] Victory of Doubt.

Let us assume for a moment the validity of the skeptical standpoint: granted that there is no metaphysical world, and that all the metaphysical explanations of the only world we know are useless to us, how would we then contemplate men and things? [Menschen und Dinge]. This can be thought out and it is worth while doing so, even if the question whether anything metaphysical has ever been demonstrated by or through Kant and Schopenhauer, be put altogether aside. For it is, to all appearances, highly probable that men, on this point, will be, in the mass, skeptical. The question thus becomes: what sort of a notion will human society, under the influence of such a state of mind, form of itself? Perhaps the *scientific demonstration* of any metaphysical world is now so difficult that mankind will never be free from a distrust of it. And when there is formed a feeling of distrust of metaphysics, the results are, in the mass, the same as if metaphysics were refuted altogether and *could* no longer be believed. In both cases the historical question, with regard to an unmetaphysical disposition in mankind, remains the same.

22
Disbelief in the "monumentum aere perennius"[*]

A decided disadvantage, attending the termination of metaphysical modes of thought, is that the individual fixes his mind too attentively upon his own brief lifetime and feels no strong inducement to aid in the foundation of institutions capable of enduring for centuries. He wishes himself to gather the fruit from the tree that he plants and consequently he no longer plants those trees which require centuries of constant cultivation and are destined to afford shade to generation after generation in the future. For metaphysical views inspire the belief that in them

---
[*] Monument more enduring than brass. Horace, Odes III:XXX.

is afforded the final sure foundation upon which henceforth the whole future of mankind may rest and be built up: the individual promotes his own salvation; when, for example, he builds a church or a monastery he is of opinion that he is doing something for the salvation of his immortal soul:—Can science, as well, inspire such faith in the efficacy of her results? In actual fact, science requires doubt and distrust as her surest auxiliaries; nevertheless, the sum of the irresistible (that is all the onslaughts of skepticism, all the disintegrating effects of surviving truths) can easily become so great (as, for instance, in the case of hygienic science) as to inspire the determination to build "eternal" works upon it. At present the contrast between our excitated ephemeral existence and the tranquil repose of metaphysical epochs is too great because both are as yet in too close juxtaposition. The individual man himself now goes through too many stages of inner and outer evolution for him to venture to make a plan even for his life time alone. A perfectly modern man, indeed, who wants to build himself a house feels as if he were walling himself up alive in a mausoleum.

23
Age of Comparison

The less men are bound by tradition, the greater is the inner activity of motives, the greater, correspondingly, the outer restlessness, the promiscuous flow of humanity, the polyphony of strivings. Who now feels any great impulse to establish himself and his posterity in a particular place? For whom, moreover, does there exist, at present, any strong tie? As all the methods of the arts were copied from one another, so were all the methods and advancements of moral codes, of manners, of civilizations.—Such an age derives its significance from the fact that in it the various ideas, codes, manners and civilizations can be compared and experienced side by side; which was impossible at an earlier period in view of the localised nature of the rule of every civilization, corresponding to the limitation of all artistic effects by time and place. To-day the growth of the aesthetic feeling is decided, owing to the great number of [artistic] forms which offer themselves for comparison. The majority—those that are condemned by the method of comparison—will be allowed to die out. In the same way there is to-day taking place a selection of the forms and customs of the higher morality which can result only in the extinction of the vulgar moralities. This is the age of comparison! That is its glory—but also its pain. Let us not, however shrink from this pain. Rather would we comprehend the nature of the task imposed upon us by our age as adequately as we can: posterity will bless us for doing so—a posterity that knows itself to be [developed] through and above the narrow, early race-civilizations as well as the culture civilization of comparison, but yet looks gratefully back upon both as venerable monuments of antiquity.

24
Possibility of Progress

When a master of the old civilization (den alten Cultur) vows to hold no more discussion with men who believe in progress, he is quite right. For the old civilization[*] has its greatness and its advantages behind it, and historic training forces one to acknowledge that it can never again acquire vigor: only intolerable stupidity or equally intolerable fanaticism could fail to perceive this fact. But men may consciously determine to evolve to a new civilization where formerly they evolved unconsciously and accidentally. They can now devise better conditions for the advancement of mankind, for their nourishment, training and education, they can administer the earth as an economic power, and, particularly, compare the capacities of men and select them accordingly. This new, conscious civilization is killing the other which, on the whole, has led but an unreflective animal and plant life: it is also destroying the doubt of progress itself—progress is possible. I mean: it is hasty and almost unreflective to assume

---

[*] Cultur, culture, civilisation etc., but there is no exact English equivalent.

that progress must *necessarily* take place: but how can it be doubted that progress is possible? On the other hand, progress in the sense and along the lines of the old civilization is not even conceivable. If romantic fantasy employs the word progress in connection with certain aims and ends identical with those of the circumscribed primitive national civilizations, the picture presented of progress is always borrowed from the past. The idea and the image of progress thus formed are quite without originality.

25
Private Ethics and World Ethics

Since the extinction of the belief that a god guides the general destiny of the world and, notwithstanding all the contortions and windings of the path of mankind, leads it gloriously forward, men must shape oecumenical, world-embracing ends for themselves. The older ethics, namely Kant's, required of the individual such a course of conduct as he wishes all men to follow. This evinces much simplicity—as if any individual could determine off hand what course of conduct would conduce to the welfare of humanity, and what course of conduct is preëminently desirable! This is a theory like that of freedom of competition, which takes it for granted that the general harmony [of things] *must* prevail of itself in accordance with some inherent law of betterment or amelioration. It may be that a later contemplation of the needs of mankind will reveal that it is by no means desirable that all men should regulate their conduct according to the same principle; it may be best, from the standpoint of certain ends yet to be attained, that men, during long periods should regulate their conduct with reference to special, and even, in certain circumstances, evil, objects. At any rate, if mankind is not to be led astray by such a universal rule of conduct, it behooves it to attain a *knowledge of the condition of culture* that will serve as a scientific standard of comparison in connection with cosmical ends. Herein is comprised the tremendous mission of the great spirits of the next century.

FRIEDRICH NIETZSCHE

26
Reaction as Progress

Occasionally harsh, powerful, impetuous, yet nevertheless backward spirits, appear, who try to conjure back some past era in the history of mankind: they serve as evidence that the new tendencies which they oppose, are not yet potent enough, that there is something lacking in them: otherwise they [the tendencies] would better withstand the effects of this conjuring back process. Thus Luther's reformation shows that in his century all the impulses to freedom of the spirit were still uncertain, lacking in vigor, and immature. Science could not yet rear her head. Indeed the whole Renaissance appears but as an early spring smothered in snow. But even in the present century Schopenhauer's metaphysic shows that the scientific spirit is not yet powerful enough: for the whole mediaeval Christian world-standpoint (Weltbetrachtung) and conception of man (Mensch-Empfindung)* once again, notwithstanding the slowly wrought destruction of all Christian dogma, celebrated a resurrection in Schopenhauer's doctrine. There is much science in his teaching although the science does not dominate, but, instead of it, the old, trite "metaphysical necessity." It is one of the greatest and most priceless advantages of Schopenhauer's teaching that by it our feelings are temporarily forced back to those old human and cosmical standpoints to which no other path could conduct us so easily. The gain for history and justice is very great. I believe that without Schopenhauer's aid it would be no easy matter for anyone now to do justice to Christianity and its Asiatic relatives— a thing impossible as regards the christianity that still survives. After according this great triumph to justice, after we have corrected in so essential a respect the historical point of view which the age of learning brought with it, we may begin to bear still farther onward the banner of enlightenment —a banner bearing the three names: Petrarch, Erasmus, Voltaire. We have

---

* Literally man-feeling or human outlook.

taken a forward step out of reaction.

27
A Substitute for Religion

It is supposed to be a recommendation for philosophy to say of it that it provides the people with a substitute for religion. And in fact, the training of the intellect does necessitate the convenient laying out of the track of thought, since the transition from religion by way of science entails a powerful, perilous leap,—something that should be advised against. With this qualification, the recommendation referred to is a just one. At the same time, it should be further explained that the needs which religion satisfies and which science must now satisfy, are not immutable. Even they can be diminished and uprooted. Think, for instance, of the christian soul-need, the sighs over one's inner corruption, the anxiety regarding salvation—all notions that arise simply out of errors of the reason and require no satisfaction at all, but annihilation. A philosophy can either so affect these needs as to appease them or else put them aside altogether, for they are acquired, circumscribed needs, based upon hypotheses which those of science explode. Here, for the purpose of affording the means of transition, for the sake of lightening the spirit overburdened with feeling, art can be employed to far better purpose, as these hypotheses receive far less support from art than from a metaphysical philosophy. Then from art it is easier to go over to a really emancipating philosophical science.

28
Discredited Words

Away with the disgustingly over-used words optimism and pessimism! For the occasion for using them grows daily less; only drivelers now find them indispensably necessary. What earthly reason could anyone have for being an optimist unless he had a god to defend who *must* have created the best of all possible worlds, since he is himself all goodness and perfection?—but what thinking man has now any need for the hypothesis that there is a god?—There is also no occasion whatever for a pessimistic confession of faith, unless one has a personal interest in denouncing the advocate of god, the theologian or the theological philosopher, and maintaining the counter proposition that evil reigns, that wretchedness is more potent than joy, that the world is a piece of botch work, that phenomenon (Erscheinung) is but the manifestation of some evil spirit. But who bothers his head about the theologians any more—except the theologians themselves? Apart from all theology and its antagonism, it is manifest that the world is neither good nor bad, (to say nothing about its being the best or the worst) and that these ideas of "good" and "bad" have significance only in relation to men, indeed, are without significance at all, in view of the sense in which they are usually employed. The contemptuous and the eulogistic point of view must, in every case, be repudiated.

29
Intoxicated by the Perfume of Flowers

The ship of humanity, it is thought, acquires an ever deeper draught the more it is laden. It is believed that the more profoundly man thinks, the more exquisitely he feels, the higher the standard he sets for himself, the greater his distance from the other animals—the more he appears as a genius (Genie) among animals—the nearer he gets to the true nature of the world and to comprehension thereof: this, indeed, he really does through science, but he thinks he does it far more adequately through his religions and arts. These are, certainly, a blossoming of the world, but not, therefore, *nearer the roots of the world* than is the stalk. One cannot learn best from it the nature of the world, although nearly everyone thinks so. *Error* has made men so deep, sensitive and imaginative in order to bring forth such flowers as religions and arts. Pure apprehension would be unable to do that. Whoever should disclose to us the essence of the world would be undeceiving us most cruelly. Not the world as thing in itself but the world as idea* (as error) is rich in portent, deep, wonderful, carrying happiness and unhappiness in its womb. This result leads to a philosophy of world negation: which, at any rate, can be as well combined with a practical world affirmation as with its opposite.

30
Evil Habits in Reaching Conclusions

The most usual erroneous conclusions of men are these: a thing[17] exists, therefore it is right: Here from capacity to live is deduced fitness, from fitness, is deduced justification. So also: an opinion gives happiness, therefore it is the true one, its effect is good, therefore it is itself good and true. Here is predicated of the effect that it gives happiness, that it is good in the sense of utility, and there is likewise predicated of the cause that it is good, but good in the sense of logical validity. Conversely, the proposition would run: a thing† cannot attain success, cannot maintain itself, therefore it is evil: a belief troubles [the believer], occasions pain, therefore it is false. The free spirit, who is sensible of the defect in this method of reaching conclusions and has had to suffer its consequences, often succumbs to the temptation to come to the very opposite conclusions (which, in general, are, of course, equally erroneous): a thing cannot maintain itself: therefore it is good; a belief is troublesome, therefore it is true.

31
The Illogical is Necessary

Among the things which can bring a thinker to distraction is the knowledge that the illogical is necessary to mankind and that

---

* Vorstellung: this word sometimes corresponds to the English word "idea", at others to "conception" or "notion."
† Sache, thing but not in the sense of Ding. Sache is of very indefinite application (res).

from the illogical springs much that is good. The illogical is so imbedded in the passions, in language, in art, in religion and, above all, in everything that imparts value to life that it cannot be taken away without irreparably injuring those beautiful things. Only men of the utmost simplicity can believe that the nature man knows can be changed into a purely logical nature. Yet were there steps affording approach to this goal, how utterly everything would be lost on the way! Even the most rational man needs nature again, from time to time, that is, his illogical fundamental relation (Grundstellung) to all things.

32
Being Unjust is Essential

All judgments of the value of life are illogically developed and therefore unjust. The vice of the judgment consists, first, in the way in which the subject matter comes under observation, that is, very incompletely; secondly in the way in which the total is summed up; and, thirdly, in the fact that each single item in the totality of the subject matter is itself the result of defective perception, and this from absolute necessity. No practical knowledge of a man, for example, stood he never so near to us, can be complete—so that we could have a logical right to form a total estimate of him; all estimates are summary and must be so. Then the standard by which we measure, (our being) is not an immutable quantity; we have moods and variations, and yet we should know ourselves as an invariable standard before we undertake to establish the nature of the relation of any thing (Sache) to ourselves. Perhaps it will follow from all this that one should form no judgments whatever; if one could but merely *live* without having to form estimates, without aversion and without partiality!—for everything most abhorred is closely connected with an estimate, as well as every strongest partiality. An inclination towards a thing, or from a thing, without an accompanying feeling that the beneficial is desired and the pernicious contemned, an inclination without a sort of experiential estimation of the desirability of an end, does not exist in man. We are primordially illogical and hence unjust beings *and can recognise this fact*: this is one of the greatest and most baffling discords of existence.

33
Error Respecting Living for the Sake of Living Essential

Every belief in the value and worthiness of life rests upon defective thinking; it is for this reason alone possible that sympathy with the general life and suffering of mankind is so imperfectly developed in the individual. Even exceptional men, who can think beyond their own personalities, do not have this general life in view, but isolated portions of it. If one is capable of fixing his observation upon exceptional cases, I mean upon highly endowed individuals and pure souled beings, if their development is taken as the true end of world-evolution and if joy be felt in their existence, then it is possible to believe in the value of life, because in that case the rest of humanity is overlooked: hence we have here defective thinking. So, too, it is even if all mankind be taken into consideration, and one species only of impulses (the less egoistic) brought under review and those, in consideration of the other impulses, exalted: then something could still be hoped of mankind in the mass and to that extent there could exist belief in the value of life: here, again, as a result of defective thinking. Whatever attitude, thus, one may assume, one is, as a result of this attitude, an exception among mankind. Now, the great majority of mankind endure life without any great protest, and believe, to this extent, in the value of existence, but that is because each individual decides and determines alone, and never comes out of his own personality like these exceptions: everything outside of the personal has no existence for them or at the utmost is observed as but a faint shadow. Consequently the value of life for the generality of mankind consists simply in the fact that the individual attaches more importance to himself than he does to the world. The great lack of imagination from which he suffers is responsible for his inability to enter into the feelings of beings other than himself, and hence his sympathy with their fate and suffering is of the slightest possible description. On the other hand, whosoever really *could* sympathise, necessarily doubts the value of life; were it possible for him to sum up and to feel in himself the total consciousness of mankind, he would collapse with a malediction against existence,—for mankind is, in the mass, without a goal, and hence man cannot find, in the contemplation of his whole course, anything to serve him as a mainstay and a comfort, but rather a reason to despair. If he looks beyond the things that immediately engage him to the final aimlessness of humanity, his own conduct assumes in his eyes the character of a frittering away. To feel oneself, however, as humanity (not alone as an individual) frittered away exactly as we see the stray leaves frittered away by nature, is a feeling transcending all feeling. But who is capable of it? Only a poet, certainly: and poets always know how to console themselves.

34
For Tranquility

But will not our philosophy become thus a tragedy? Will not truth prove the enemy of life, of betterment? A question seems to weigh upon our tongue and yet will not put itself into words: whether one *can* knowingly remain in the domain of the untruthful? or, if one *must*, whether, then, death would not be preferable? For there is no longer any ought (Sollen), morality; so far as it is involved "ought," is, through our point of view, as utterly annihilated as religion. Our knowledge can permit only pleasure and pain, benefit and injury, to subsist as motives. But how can these motives be distinguished from the desire for truth? Even they rest upon error (in so far, as already stated, partiality and dislike and their very inaccurate estimates palpably modify our pleasure and our pain). The whole of human life is deeply involved in *untruth*. The individual cannot extricate it from this pit without thereby fundamentally clashing with his whole past, without finding his present motives of conduct, (as that of honor) illegitimate, and without opposing scorn and contempt to the ambitions which prompt one to have regard for the future and for one's happiness in the future. Is it true, does there, then, remain but one way of thinking, which, as a personal consequence brings in its train despair, and as a theoretical [consequence brings in its train] a philosophy of decay, disintegration, self annihilation? I believe the deciding influence, as regards the after-effect of knowledge, will be the *temperament* of a man; I can, in addition to this after-effect just mentioned, suppose another, by means of which a much simpler life, and one freer from disturbances than the present, could be lived; so that at first the old motives of vehement passion might still have strength, owing to hereditary habit, but they would gradually grow weaker under the influence of purifying knowledge. A man would live, at last, both among men and unto himself, as in the natural state, without praise, reproach, competition, feasting one's eyes, as if it were a play, upon much that formerly inspired dread. One would be rid of the strenuous element, and would no longer feel the goad of the reflection that man is not even [as much as] nature, nor more than nature. To be sure, this requires, as already stated, a good temperament, a fortified, gentle and naturally cheerful soul, a disposition that has no need to be on its guard against its own eccentricities and sudden outbreaks and that in its utterances manifests neither sullenness nor a snarling tone—those familiar, disagreeable characteristics of old dogs and old men that have been a long time chained up. Rather must a man, from whom the ordinary bondages of life have fallen away to so great an extent, so do that he only lives on in order to grow continually in knowledge, and to learn to resign, without envy and without disappointment, much, yes nearly everything, that has value in the eyes of men. He must be content with such a free, fearless soaring above men, manners, laws and traditional estimates of things, as the most desirable of all situations. He will freely share the joy of being in such a situation, and he has, perhaps, nothing else to share—in which renunciation and self-denial really most consist. But if more is asked of him, he will, with a benevolent shake of the head, refer to his brother, the free man of fact, and will, perhaps, not dissemble a little contempt: for, as regards his "freedom," thereby hangs a tale.*

---

* den mit dessen "Freiheit" hat es eine eigene Bewandtniss.

HISTORY OF THE MORAL FEELINGS

35
Advantages of Psychological Observation

That reflection regarding the human, all-too-human—or as the learned jargon is: psychological observation—is among the means whereby the burden of life can be made lighter, that practice in this art affords presence of mind in difficult situations and entertainment amid a wearisome environment, aye, that maxims may be culled in the thorniest and least pleasing paths of life and invigoration thereby obtained: this much was believed, was known—in former centuries. Why was this forgotten in our own century, during which, at least in Germany, yes in Europe, poverty as regards psychological observation would have been manifest in many ways had there been anyone to whom this poverty could have manifested itself. Not only in the novel, in the romance, in philosophical standpoints—these are the works of exceptional men; still more in the state of opinion regarding public events and personages; above all in general society, which says much about men but nothing whatever about man, there is totally lacking the art of psychological analysis and synthesis. But why is the richest and most harmless source of entertainment thus allowed to run to waste? Why is the greatest master of the psychological maxim no longer read?—for, with no exaggeration

43

whatever be it said: the educated person in Europe who has read La Rochefoucauld and his intellectual and artistic affinities is very hard to find; still harder, the person who knows them and does not disparage them. Apparently, too, this unusual reader takes far less pleasure in them than the form adopted by these artists should afford him: for the subtlest mind cannot adequately appreciate the art of maxim-making unless it has had training in it, unless it has competed in it. Without such practical acquaintance, one is apt to look upon this making and forming as a much easier thing than it really is; one is not keenly enough alive to the felicity and the charm of success. Hence present day readers of maxims have but a moderate, tempered pleasure in them, scarcely, indeed, a true perception of their merit, so that their experiences are about the same as those of the average beholder of cameos: people who praise because they cannot appreciate, and are very ready to admire and still readier to turn away.

36
Objection

Or is there a counter-proposition to the dictum that psychological observation is one of the means of consoling, lightening, charming existence? Have enough of the unpleasant effects of this art been experienced to justify the person striving for culture in turning his regard away from it? In all truth, a certain blind faith in the goodness of human nature, an implanted distaste for any disparagement of human concerns, a sort of shamefacedness at the nakedness of the soul, may be far more desirable things in the general happiness of a man, than this only occasionally advantageous quality of psychological sharpsightedness; and perhaps belief in the good, in virtuous men and actions, in a plenitude of disinterested benevolence has been more productive of good in the world of men in so far as it has made men less distrustful. If Plutarch's heroes are enthusiastically imitated and a reluctance is experienced to looking too critically into the motives of their actions, not the knowledge but the welfare of human society is promoted thereby: psychological error and above all obtuseness in regard to it, help human nature forward, whereas knowledge of the truth is more promoted by means of the stimulating strength of a hypothesis; as La Rochefoucauld in the first edition of his "Sentences and Moral Maxims" has expressed it: "What the world calls virtue is ordinarily but a phantom created by the passions, and to which we give a good name in order to do whatever we please with impunity." La Rochefoucauld and those other French masters of soul-searching (to the number of whom has lately been added a German, the author of "Psychological Observations") are like expert marksmen who again and again hit the black spot—but it is the black spot in human nature. Their art inspires amazement, but finally some spectator, inspired, not by the scientific spirit but by a humanitarian feeling, execrates an art that seems to implant in the soul a taste for belittling and impeaching mankind.

37
Nevertheless

The matter therefore, as regards pro and con, stands thus: in the present state of philosophy an awakening of the moral observation is essential. The repulsive aspect of psychological dissection, with the knife and tweezers entailed by the process, can no longer be spared humanity. Such is the imperative duty of any science that investigates the origin and history of the so-called moral feelings and which, in its progress, is called upon to posit and to solve advanced social problems:—The older philosophy does not recognize the newer at all and, through paltry evasions, has always gone astray in the investigation of the origin and history of human estimates (Werthschätzungen). With what results may now be very clearly perceived, since it has been shown by many examples, how the errors of the greatest philosophers have their origin in a false explanation of certain human actions and feelings; how upon the foundation of an erroneous analysis (for example, of the so called disinterested actions), a false ethic is reared, to support which religion and like mythological monstrosities are called in, until finally the shades of these troubled spirits collapse in physics and in the comprehensive world point of view. But if it be established that superficiality of psychological observation has heretofore set the most dangerous snares for human judgment and deduction, and will continue to do so, all the greater need is there of that steady continuance of labor that never wearies putting stone upon stone, little stone upon little stone; all the greater need is there of a courage that is not ashamed of such humble labor and that will oppose persistence, to all contempt. It is, finally, also true that countless single observations concerning the human, all-too-human, have been first made and uttered in circles accustomed, not to furnish matter for scientific knowledge, but for intellectual pleasure-seeking; and the original home atmosphere—a very seductive atmosphere—of the moral maxim has almost inextricably interpenetrated the entire species, so that the scientific man involuntarily manifests a sort of mistrust of this species and of its seriousness. But it is sufficient to point to the consequences: for already it is becoming evident that events of the most portentous nature are developing in the domain of psychological observation. What is the leading conclusion arrived at by one of the subtlest and calmest of thinkers, the author of the work "Concerning the Origin of the Moral Feelings", as a result of his thorough and incisive analysis of human conduct? "The moral man," he says, "stands no nearer the knowable (metaphysical) world than the physical man."* This dictum, grown hard and cutting beneath the hammer-blow of historical knowledge, can some day, perhaps, in some future or other, serve as the axe that will be laid to the root of the "metaphysical necessities" of men—whether more to the blessing than to the banning of universal well being who can say?—but in any event a dictum fraught with the most momentous consequences, fruitful and fearful at once, and confronting the world in the two faced

---

* "Der moralische Mensch, sagt er, steht der intelligiblen (metaphysischen) Welt nicht näher, als der physische Mensch."

way characteristic of all great facts.

38
To What Extent Useful

Therefore, whether psychological observation is more an advantage than a disadvantage to mankind may always remain undetermined: but there is no doubt that it is necessary, because science can no longer dispense with it. Science, however, recognizes no considerations of ultimate goals or ends any more than nature does; but as the latter duly matures things of the highest fitness for certain ends without any intention of doing it, so will true science, doing with ideas what nature does with matter,* promote the purposes and the welfare of humanity, (as occasion may afford, and in many ways) and attain fitness [to ends]—but likewise without having intended it.

He to whom the atmospheric conditions of such a prospect are too wintry, has too little fire in him: let him look about him, and he will become sensible of maladies requiring an icy air, and of people who are so "kneaded together" out of ardor and intellect that they can scarcely find anywhere an atmosphere too cold and cutting for them. Moreover: as too serious individuals and nations stand in need of trivial relaxations; as others, too volatile and excitable require onerous, weighty ordeals to render them entirely healthy: should not we, the more intellectual men of this age, which is swept more and more by conflagrations, catch up every cooling and extinguishing appliance we can find that we may always remain as self contained, steady and calm as we are now, and thereby perhaps serve this age as its mirror and self reflector, when the occasion arises?

---

* als die Nachahmung der Natur in Begriffen, literally: "as the counterfeit of nature in (regard to) ideas."

39
The Fable of Discretionary Freedom

The history of the feelings, on the basis of which we make everyone responsible, hence, the so-called moral feelings, is traceable in the following leading phases. At first single actions are termed good or bad without any reference to their motive, but solely because of the utilitarian or prejudicial consequences they have for the community. In time, however, the origin of these designations is forgotten [but] it is imagined that action in itself, without reference to its consequences, contains the property "good" or "bad": with the same error according to which language designates the stone itself as hard[ness] the tree itself as green[ness]—for the reason, therefore, that what is a consequence is comprehended as a cause. Accordingly, the good[ness] or bad[ness] is incorporated into the motive and [any] deed by itself is regarded as morally ambiguous. A step further is taken, and the predication good or bad is no longer made of the particular motives but of the entire nature of a man, out of which motive grows as grow the plants out of the soil. Thus man is successively made responsible for his [particular] acts, then for his [course of] conduct, then for his motives and finally for his nature. Now, at last, is it discovered that this nature, even, cannot be responsible, inasmuch as it is only and wholly a necessary consequence and is synthesised out of the elements and influence of past and present things: therefore, that man is to be made responsible for nothing, neither for his nature, nor his motives, nor his [course of] conduct nor his [particular] acts. By this [process] is gained the knowledge that the history of moral estimates is the history of error, of the error of responsibility: as is whatever rests upon the error of the freedom of the will. Schopenhauer concluded just the other way, thus: since certain actions bring depression ("consciousness of guilt") in their train, there must, then, exist responsibility, for there would be no basis for this depression at hand if all man's affairs did not follow their course of necessity—as they do, indeed, according to the opinion of this philosopher, follow their course—but man himself, subject to the same necessity, would be just the man that he is—which Schopenhauer denies. From the fact of such depression Schopenhauer believes himself able to prove a freedom which man in some way must have had, not indeed in regard to his actions but in regard to his nature: freedom, therefore, to be thus and so, not to act thus and so. Out of the *esse*, the sphere of freedom and responsibility, follows, according to his opinion, the *operari*, the spheres of invariable causation, necessity and irresponsibility. This depression, indeed, is due apparently to the *operari*—in so far as it be delusive—but in truth to whatever *esse* be the deed of a free will, the basic cause of the existence of an individual: [in order to] let man become whatever he wills to become, his [to] will (Wollen) must precede his existence.—Here, apart from the absurdity of the statement just made, there is drawn the wrong inference that the fact of the depression explains its character, the rational admissibility of it: from such a wrong inference does Schopenhauer first come to his fantastic consequent of the so called discretionary freedom (intelligibeln Freiheit). (For the origin of this fabulous entity Plato and Kant are equally responsible). But depression after the act does not need to be rational: indeed, it is certainly not so at all, for it rests upon the erroneous assumption that the act need not necessarily have come to pass. Therefore: only because man deems himself free, but not because he is free, does he experience remorse and the stings of conscience.—Moreover, this depression is something that can be grown out of; in many men it is not present at all as a consequence of acts which inspire it in many other men. It is a very varying thing and one closely connected with the development of custom and civilization, and perhaps manifest only during a relatively brief period of the world's history.—No one is responsible for his acts, no one for his nature; to judge is tantamount to being unjust. This applies as well when the individual judges himself. The proposition is as clear as sunlight, and yet here everyone prefers to go back to darkness and untruth: for fear of the consequences.

40
Above Animal

The beast in us must be wheedled: ethic is necessary, that we may not be torn to pieces. Without the errors involved in the assumptions of ethics, man would have remained an animal. Thus has he taken himself as something higher and imposed rigid laws upon himself. He feels hatred, consequently, for states approximating the animal: whence the former contempt for the slave as a not-yet-man, as a thing, is to be explained.

41
Unalterable Character

That character is unalterable is not, in the strict sense, true; rather is this favorite proposition valid only to the extent that during the brief life period of a man the potent new motives can not, usually, press down hard enough to obliterate the lines imprinted by ages. Could we conceive of a man eighty thousand years old, we should have in him an absolutely alterable character; so that the maturities of successive, varying individuals would develop in him. The shortness of human life leads to many erroneous assertions concerning the qualities of man.

42
Classification of Enjoyments and Ethic

The once accepted comparative classification of enjoyments, according to which an inferior, higher, highest egoism may crave one or another enjoyment, now decides as to ethical status or unethical status. A lower enjoyment (for example, sensual pleasure) preferred to a more highly esteemed one (for example, health) rates as unethical, as does welfare preferred to freedom. The comparative classification of enjoyments is not, however, alike or the same at all periods; when anyone demands satisfaction of the law, he is, from the point of view of an earlier civilization, moral, from that of the present, non-moral.

"Unethical" indicates, therefore, that a man is not sufficiently sensible to the higher, finer impulses which the present civilization has brought with it, or is not sensible to them at all; it indicates backwardness, but only from the point of view of the contemporary degree of distinction.—The comparative classification of enjoyments itself is not determined according to absolute ethics; but after each new ethical adjustment, it is then decided whether conduct be ethical or the reverse.

43
Inhuman Men as Survivals

Men who are now inhuman must serve us as surviving specimens of earlier civilizations. The mountain height of humanity here reveals its lower formations, which might otherwise remain hidden from view. There are surviving specimens of humanity whose brains through the vicissitudes of heredity, have escaped proper development. They show us what we all were and thus appal us; but they are as little responsible on this account as is a piece of granite for being granite. In our own brains there must be courses and windings corresponding to such characters, just as in the forms of some human organs there survive traces of fishhood. But these courses and windings are no longer the bed in which flows the stream of our feeling.

44
Gratitude and Revenge

The reason the powerful man is grateful is this. His benefactor has, through his benefaction, invaded the domain of the powerful man and established himself on an equal footing: the powerful man in turn invades the domain of the benefactor and gets satisfaction through the act of gratitude. It is a mild form of revenge. By not obtaining the satisfaction of gratitude the powerful would have shown himself powerless and have ranked as such thenceforward. Hence every society of the good, that is to say, of the powerful originally, places gratitude among the first of duties.—Swift has added the dictum that man is grateful in the same degree that he is revengeful.

45
Two-fold Historical Origin of Good and Evil

The notion of good and bad has a two-fold historical origin: namely, first, in the spirit of ruling races and castes. Whoever has power to requite good with good and evil with evil and actually brings requital, (that is, is grateful and revengeful) acquires the name of being good; whoever is powerless and cannot requite is called bad. A man belongs, as a good individual, to the "good" of a community, who have a feeling in common, because all the individuals are allied with one another through the requiting sentiment. A man belongs, as a bad individual, to the "bad," to a mass of subjugated, powerless men who have no feeling in common. The good are a caste, the bad are a quantity, like dust. Good and bad is, for a considerable period, tantamount to noble and servile, master and slave. On the other hand an enemy is not looked upon as bad: he can requite. The Trojan and the Greek are in Homer both good. Not he, who does no harm, but he who is despised, is deemed bad. In the community of the good individuals [the quality of] good[ness] is inherited; it is impossible for a bad individual to grow from such a rich soil. If, notwithstanding, one of the good individuals does something unworthy of his goodness, recourse is had to exorcism; thus the guilt is ascribed to a deity, the while it is declared that this deity bewitched the good man into madness and blindness.—Second, in the spirit of the subjugated, the powerless. Here every other man is, to the individual, hostile, inconsiderate, greedy, inhuman, avaricious, be he noble or servile; bad is the characteristic term for man, for every living being, indeed, that is recognized at all, even for a god: human, divine, these notions are tantamount to devilish, bad. Manifestations of goodness, sympathy, helpfulness, are regarded with anxiety as trickiness, preludes to an evil end, deception, subtlety, in short, as refined badness. With such a predisposition in individuals, a feeling in common can scarcely arise at all, at most only the rudest form of it: so that everywhere that this conception of good and evil prevails, the destruction of the individuals, their race and nation, is imminent.—Our existing morality has developed upon the foundation laid by ruling races and castes.

46
Sympathy Greater than Suffering.

There are circumstances in which sympathy is stronger than the suffering itself. We feel more pain, for instance, when one of our friends becomes guilty of a reprehensible action than if we had done the deed ourselves. We once, that is, had more faith in the purity of his character than he had himself. Hence our love for him, (apparently because of this very faith) is stronger than is his own love for himself. If, indeed, his egoism really suffers more, as a result, than our egoism, inasmuch as he must take the consequences of his fault to a greater extent than ourselves, nevertheless, the unegoistic—this word is not to be taken too strictly, but simply as a modified form of expression—in us is more affected by his guilt than the unegoistic in him.

47
Hypochondria

There are people who, from sympathy and anxiety for others become hypochondriacal. The resulting form of compassion is nothing else than sickness. So, also, is there a Christian hypochondria, from which those singular, religiously agitated people suffer who place always before their eyes the suffering and death of Christ.

48
Economy of Blessings

The advantageous and the pleasing, as the healthiest growths and powers in the intercourse of men, are such precious treasures that it is much to be wished the use made of these balsamic means were as economical as possible: but this is impossible. Economy in the use of blessings is the dream of the craziest of Utopians.

49
Well-Wishing

Among the small, but infinitely plentiful and therefore very potent things to which science must pay more attention than to the great, uncommon things, well-wishing* must be reckoned; I mean those manifestations of friendly disposition in intercourse, that laughter of the eye, every hand pressure, every courtesy from which, in general, every human act gets its quality. Every teacher, every functionary adds this element as a gratuity to whatever he does as a duty; it is the perpetual well spring of humanity, like the waves of light in which everything grows; thus, in the narrowest circles, within the family, life blooms and flowers only through this kind feeling. The cheerfulness, friendliness and kindness of a heart are unfailing sources of unegoistic impulse and have made far more for civilization than those other more noised manifestations of it that are styled sympathy, benevolence and sacrifice. But it is customary to depreciate these little tokens of kindly feeling, and, indeed, there is not much of the unegoistic in them. The sum of these little doses is very great, nevertheless; their combined strength is of the greatest of strengths.—Thus, too, much more happiness is to be found in the world than gloomy eyes discover: that is, if the calculation be just, and all these pleasing moments in which every day, even the meanest human life, is rich, be not forgotten.

---

* Wohl-wollen, kind feeling. It stands here for benevolence but not benevolence in the restricted sense of the word now prevailing.

FRIEDRICH NIETZSCHE

50
The Desire to Inspire Compassion

La Rochefoucauld, in the most notable part of his self portraiture (first printed 1658) reaches the vital spot of truth when he warns all those endowed with reason to be on their guard against compassion, when he advises that this sentiment be left to men of the masses who stand in need of the promptings of the emotions (since they are not guided by reason) to induce them to give aid to the suffering and to be of service in misfortune: whereas compassion, in his (and Plato's) view, deprives the heart of strength. To be sure, sympathy should be manifested but men should take care not to feel it; for the unfortunate are rendered so dull that the manifestation of sympathy affords them the greatest happiness in the world.—Perhaps a more effectual warning against this compassion can be given if this need of the unfortunate be considered not simply as stupidity and intellectual weakness, not as a sort of distraction of the spirit entailed by misfortune itself (and thus, indeed, does La Rochefoucauld seem to view it) but as something quite different and more momentous. Let note be taken of children who cry and scream in order to be compassionated and who, therefore, await the moment when their condition will be observed; come into contact with the sick and the oppressed in spirit and try to ascertain if the wailing and sighing, the posturing and posing of misfortune do not have as end and aim the causing of pain to the beholder: the sympathy which each beholder manifests is a consolation to the weak and suffering only in as much as they are made to perceive that at least they have the power, notwithstanding all their weakness, to inflict pain. The unfortunate experiences a species of joy in the sense of superiority which the manifestation of sympathy entails; his imagination is exalted; he is always strong enough, then, to cause the world pain. Thus is the thirst for sympathy a thirst for self enjoyment and at the expense of one's fellow creatures: it shows man in the whole ruthlessness of his own dear self, not in his mere "dullness" as La Rochefoucauld thinks.—In social conversation three fourths of all the questions are asked, and three fourths of all the replies are made in order to inflict some little pain; that is why so many people crave social intercourse: it gives them a sense of their power. In these countless but very small doses in which the quality of badness is administered it proves a potent stimulant of life: to the same extent that well wishing—(Wohl-wollen) distributed through the world in like manner, is one of the ever ready restoratives.—But will many honorable people be found to admit that there is any pleasure in administering pain? that entertainment—and rare entertainment—is not seldom found in causing others, at least in thought, some pain, and in raking them with the small shot of wickedness? The majority are too ignoble and a few are too good to know anything of this pudendum: the latter may, consequently, be prompt to deny that Prosper Mérimée is right when he says: "Know, also, that nothing is more common than to do wrong for the pleasure of doing it."

51
How Appearance Becomes Reality

The actor cannot, at last, refrain, even in moments of the deepest pain, from thinking of the effect produced by his deportment and by his surroundings—for example, even at the funeral of his own child: he will weep at his own sorrow and its manifestations as though he were his own audience. The hypocrite who always plays one and the same part, finally ceases to be a hypocrite; as in the case of priests who, when young men, are always, either consciously or unconsciously, hypocrites, and finally become naturally and then really, without affectation, mere priests: or if the father does not carry it to this extent, the son, who inherits his father's calling and gets the advantage of the paternal progress, does. When anyone, during a long period, and persistently, wishes to appear something, it will at last prove difficult for him to be anything else. The calling of almost every man, even of the artist, begins with hypocrisy, with an imitation of deportment, with a copying of the effective in manner. He who always wears the mask of a friendly man must at last gain a power over friendliness of disposition, without which the expression itself of friendliness is not to be gained—and finally friendliness of disposition gains the ascendancy over him—he *is* benevolent.

52
The Point of Honor in Deception

In all great deceivers one characteristic is prominent, to which they owe their power. In the very act of deception, amid all the accompaniments, the agitation in the voice, the expression, the bearing, in the crisis of the scene, there comes over them a belief in themselves; this it is that acts so effectively and irresistibly upon the beholders. Founders of religions differ from such great deceivers in that they never come out of this state of self deception, or else they have, very rarely, a few moments of enlightenment in which they are overcome by doubt; generally, however, they soothe themselves by ascribing such moments of enlightenment to the evil adversary. Self deception must exist that both classes of deceivers may attain far reaching results. For men believe in the truth of all that is manifestly believed with due implicitness by others.

53
Presumed Degrees of Truth

One of the most usual errors of deduction is: because someone truly and openly is against us, therefore he speaks the truth. Hence the child has faith in the judgments of its elders, the Christian in the assertions of the founder of the church. So, too, it will not be admitted that all for which men sacrificed life and happiness in former centuries was nothing but delusion: perhaps it is alleged these things were degrees of truth. But what is really meant is that, if a person sincerely believes a thing and has fought and died for his faith, it would be too *unjust* if only delusion had inspired him. Such a state of affairs seems to contradict eternal justice. For that reason the heart of a sensitive man pronounces against his head the judgment: between moral conduct and intellectual insight there must always exist an inherent connection. It is, unfortunately, otherwise: for there is no eternal justice.

54
Falsehood

Why do men, as a rule, speak the truth in the ordinary affairs of life? Certainly not for the reason that a god has forbidden lying. But because first: it is more convenient, as falsehood entails invention, make-believe and recollection (wherefore Swift says that whoever invents a lie seldom realises the heavy burden he takes up: he must, namely, for every lie that he tells, insert twenty more). Therefore, because in plain ordinary relations of life it is expedient to say without circumlocution: I want this, I have done this, and the like; therefore, because the way of freedom and certainty is surer than that of ruse.—But if it happens that a child is brought up in sinister domestic circumstances, it will then indulge in falsehood as matter of course, and involuntarily say anything its own interests may prompt: an inclination for truth, an aversion to falsehood, is quite foreign and uncongenial to it, and hence it lies in all innocence.

55
Ethic Discredited for Faith's Sake

No power can sustain itself when it is represented by mere humbugs: the Catholic Church may possess ever so many "worldly" sources of strength, but its true might is comprised in those still numberless priestly natures who make their lives stern and strenuous and whose looks and emaciated bodies are eloquent of night vigils, fasts, ardent prayer, perhaps even of whip lashes: these things make men tremble and cause them anxiety: what, if it be really imperative to live thus? This is the dreadful question which their aspect occasions. As they spread this doubt, they lay anew the prop of their power: even the free thinkers dare not oppose such disinterestedness with severe truth and cry: "Thou deceived one, deceive not!"—Only the difference of standpoint separates them from him: no difference in goodness or badness. But things we cannot accomplish ourselves, we are apt to criticise unfairly. Thus we are told of the cunning and perverted acts of the Jesuits, but we overlook the self mastery that each Jesuit imposes upon himself and also the fact that the easy life which the Jesuit manuals advocate is for the benefit, not of the Jesuits but the laity. Indeed, it may be questioned whether we enlightened ones would become equally competent workers as the result of similar tactics and organization, and equally worthy of admiration as the result of self mastery, indefatigable industry and devotion.

56
Victory of Knowledge over Radical Evil

It proves a material gain to him who would attain knowledge to have had during a considerable period the idea that mankind is a radically bad and perverted thing: it is a false idea, as is its opposite, but it long held sway and its roots have reached down even to ourselves and our present world. In order to understand *ourselves* we must understand *it*; but in order to attain a loftier height we must step above it. We then perceive that there is no such thing as sin in the metaphysical sense: but also, in the same sense, no such thing as virtue; that this whole domain of ethical notions is one of constant variation; that there are higher and deeper conceptions of good and evil, moral and immoral. Whoever desires no more of things than knowledge of them attains speedily to peace of mind and will at most err through lack of knowledge, but scarcely through eagerness for knowledge (or through sin, as the world calls it). He will not ask that eagerness for knowledge be interdicted and rooted out; but his single, all powerful ambition to *know* as thoroughly and as fully as possible, will soothe him and moderate all that is strenuous in his circumstances. Moreover, he is now rid of a number of disturbing notions; he is no longer beguiled by such words as hell-pain, sinfulness, unworthiness: he sees in them merely the flitting shadow pictures of false views of life and of the world.

57
Ethic as Man's Self-Analysis

A good author, whose heart is really in his work, wishes that someone would arise and wholly refute him if only thereby his subject be wholly clarified and made plain. The maid in love wishes that she could attest the fidelity of her own passion through the faithlessness of her beloved. The soldier wishes to sacrifice his life on the field of his fatherland's victory: for in the victory of his fatherland his highest end is attained. The mother gives her child what she deprives herself of—sleep, the best nourishment and, in certain circumstances, her health, her self.— But are all these acts unegoistic? Are these moral deeds miracles because they are, in Schopenhauer's phrase "impossible and yet accomplished"? Is it not evident that in all four cases man loves one part of himself, (a thought, a longing, an experience) more than he loves another part of himself? that he thus analyses his being and sacrifices one part of it to another part? Is this essentially different from the behavior of the obstinate man who says "I would rather be shot than go a step out of my way for this fellow"?—Preference for something (wish, impulse, longing) is present in all four instances: to yield to it, with all its consequences, is not "unegoistic."—In the domain of the ethical man conducts himself not as individuum but as dividuum.

58
What Can be Promised

Actions can be promised, but not feelings, for these are involuntary. Whoever promises somebody to love him always, or to hate him always, or to be ever true to him, promises something that it is out of his power to bestow. But he really can promise such courses of conduct as are the ordinary accompaniments of love, of hate, of fidelity, but which may also have their source in motives quite different: for various ways and motives lead to the same conduct. The promise to love someone always, means, consequently: as long as I love you, I will manifest the deportment of love; but if I cease to love you my deportment, although from some other motive, will be just the same, so that to the people about us it will seem as if my love remained unchanged.—Hence it is the continuance of the deportment of love that is promised in every instance in which eternal love (provided no element of self deception be involved) is sworn.

59
Intellect and Ethic

One must have a good memory to be able to keep the promises one makes. One must have a strong imagination in order to feel sympathy. So closely is ethics connected with intellectual capacity.

60
Desire for Vengeance and Vengeance Itself

To meditate revenge and attain it is tantamount to an attack of fever, that passes away: but to meditate revenge without possessing the strength or courage to attain it is tantamount to suffering from a chronic malady, or poisoning of body and soul. Ethics, which takes only the motive into account, rates both cases alike: people generally estimate the first case as the worst (because of the consequences which the deed of vengeance may entail). Both views are short sighted.

61
Ability to Wait

Ability to wait is so hard to acquire that great poets have not disdained to make inability to wait the central motive of their poems. So Shakespeare in Othello, Sophocles in Ajax, whose suicide would not have seemed to him so imperative had he only been able to cool his ardor for a day, as the oracle foreboded: apparently he would then have repulsed somewhat the fearful whispers of distracted thought and have said to himself: Who has not already, in my situation, mistaken a sheep for a hero? is it so extraordinary a thing? On the contrary it is something universally human: Ajax should thus have soothed himself. Passion will not wait: the tragic element in the lives of great men does not generally consist in their conflict with time and the inferiority of their fellowmen but in their inability to put off their work a year or two: they cannot wait.—In all duels, the friends who advise have but to ascertain if the principals can wait: if this be not possible, a duel is rational inasmuch as each of the combatants may say: "either I continue to live and the other dies instantly, or vice versa." To wait in such circumstances would be equivalent to the frightful martyrdom of enduring dishonor in the presence of him responsible for the dishonor: and this can easily cost more anguish than life is worth.

62
Glutting Revenge

Coarse men, who feel a sense of injury, are in the habit of rating the extent of their injury as high as possible and of stating the occasion of it in greatly exaggerated language, in order to be able to feast themselves on the sentiments of hatred and revenge thus aroused.

63
Value of Disparagement

Not a few, perhaps the majority of men, find it necessary, in order to retain their self esteem and a certain uprightness in conduct, to mentally disparage and belittle all the people they know. But as the inferior natures are in the majority and as a great deal depends upon whether they retain or lose this uprightness, so—

64
The Man in a Rage

We should be on our guard against the man who is enraged against us, as against one who has attempted our life, for the fact that we still live consists solely in the inability to kill: were looks sufficient, it would have been all up with us long since. To reduce anyone to silence by physical manifestations of savagery or by a terrorizing process is a relic of under civilization. So, too, that cold look which great personages cast upon their servitors is a remnant of the caste distinction between man and man; a specimen of rude antiquity: women, the conservers of the old, have maintained this survival, too, more perfectly than men.

65
Whither Honesty May Lead

Someone once had the bad habit of expressing himself upon occasion, and with perfect honesty, on the subject of the motives of his conduct, which were as good or as bad as the motives of all men. He aroused first disfavor, then suspicion, became gradually of ill repute and was pronounced a person of whom society should beware, until at last the law took note of such a perverted being for reasons which usually have no weight with it or to which it closes its eyes. Lack of taciturnity concerning what is universally held secret, and an irresponsible predisposition to see what no one wants to see—oneself—brought him to prison and to early death.

66
Punishable, not Punished

Our crime against criminals consists in the fact that we treat them as rascals,

67
Sancta simplicitas of Virtue

Every virtue has its privilege: for example, that of contributing its own little bundle of wood to the funeral pyre of one condemned.

68
Morality and Consequence

Not alone the beholders of an act generally estimate the ethical or unethical element in it by the result: no, the one who performed the act does the same. For the motives and the intentions are seldom sufficiently apparent, and amid them the memory itself seems to become clouded by the results of the act, so that a man often ascribes the wrong motives to his acts or regards the remote motives as the direct ones. Success often imparts to an action all the brilliance and honor of good intention, while failure throws the shadow of conscience over the most estimable deeds. Hence arises the familiar maxim of the politician: "Give me only success: with it I can win all the noble souls over to my side—and make myself noble even in my own eyes."—In like manner will success prove an excellent substitute for a better argument. To this very day many well educated men think the triumph of Christianity over Greek philosophy is a proof of the superior truth of the former—although in this case it was simply the coarser and more powerful that triumphed over the more delicate and intellectual. As regards superiority of truth, it is evident that because of it the reviving sciences have connected themselves, point for point, with the philosophy of Epicurus, while Christianity has, point for point, recoiled from it.

69
Love and Justice

Why is love so highly prized at the expense of justice and why are such beautiful things spoken of the former as if it were a far higher entity than the latter? Is the former not palpably a far more stupid thing than the latter?—Certainly, and on that very account so much the more agreeable to everybody: it is blind and has a rich horn of plenty out of which it distributes its gifts to everyone, even when they are unmerited, even when no thanks are returned. It is impartial like the rain, which according to the bible and experience, wets not alone the unjust but, in certain circumstances, the just as well, and to their skins at that.

70
Execution

How comes it that every execution causes us more pain than a murder? It is the coolness of the executioner, the painful preparation, the perception that here a man is being used as an instrument for the intimidation of others. For the guilt is not punished even if there be any: this is ascribable to the teachers, the parents, the environment, in ourselves, not in the murderer—I mean the predisposing circumstances.

71
Hope

Pandora brought the box containing evils and opened it. It was the gift of the gods to men, a gift of most enticing appearance externally and called the "box of happiness." Thereupon all the evils, (living, moving things) flew out: from that time to the present they fly about and do ill to men by day and night. One evil only did not fly out of the box: Pandora shut the lid at the behest of Zeus and it remained inside. Now man has this box of happiness perpetually in the house and congratulates himself upon the treasure inside of it; it is at his service: he grasps it whenever he is so disposed, for he knows not that the box which Pandora brought was a box of evils. Hence he looks upon the one evil still remaining as the greatest source of happiness—it is hope.—Zeus intended that man, notwithstanding the evils oppressing him, should continue to live and not rid himself of life, but keep on making himself miserable. For this purpose he bestowed hope upon man: it is, in truth, the greatest of evils for it lengthens the ordeal of man.

72
Degree of Moral Susceptibility Unknown

The fact that one has or has not had certain profoundly moving impressions and insights into things—for example, an unjustly executed, slain or martyred father, a faithless wife, a shattering, serious accident,—is the factor upon which the excitation of our passions to white heat principally depends, as well as the course of our whole lives. No one knows to what lengths circumstances (sympathy, emotion) may lead him. He does not know the full extent of his own susceptibility. Wretched environment makes him wretched. It is as a rule not the quality of our experience but its quantity upon which depends the development of our superiority or inferiority, from the point of view of good and evil.

73
The Martyr Against His Will

In a certain movement there was a man who was too cowardly and vacillating ever to contradict his comrades. He was made use of in each emergency, every sacrifice was demanded of him because he feared the disfavor of his comrades more than he feared death: he was a petty, abject spirit. They perceived this and upon the foundation of the qualities just mentioned they elevated him to the altitude of a hero, and finally even of a martyr. Although the cowardly creature always inwardly said No, he always said Yes with his lips, even upon the scaffold, where he died for the tenets of his party: for beside him stood one of his old associates who so domineered him with look and word that he actually went to his death with the utmost fortitude and has ever since been celebrated as a martyr and exalted character.

74
General Standard

One will rarely err if extreme actions be ascribed to vanity, ordinary actions to habit and mean actions to fear.

75
Misunderstanding of Virtue

Whoever has obtained his experience of vice in connection with pleasure as in the case of one with a youth of wild oats behind him, comes to the conclusion that virtue must be connected with self denial. Whoever, on the other hand, has been very much plagued by his passions and vices, longs to find in virtue the rest and peace of the soul. That is why it is possible for two virtuous people to misunderstand one another wholly.

76
The Ascetic

The ascetic makes out of virtue a slavery.

77
Honor Transferred from Persons to Things

Actions prompted by love or by the spirit of self sacrifice for others are universally honored wherever they are manifest. Hence is magnified the value set upon whatever things may be loved or whatever things conduce to self sacrifice: although in themselves they may be worth nothing much. A valiant army is evidence of the value of the thing it fights for.

78
Ambition a Substitute for Moral Feeling

Moral feeling should never become extinct in natures that are destitute of ambition. The ambitious can get along without moral feeling just as well as with it.—Hence the sons of retired, ambitionless families, generally become by a series of rapid gradations, when they lose moral feeling, the most absolute lunkheads.

79
Vanity Enriches

How poor the human mind would be without vanity! As it is, it resembles a well stacked and ever renewed ware-emporium that attracts buyers of every class: they can find almost everything, have almost everything, provided they bring with them the right kind of money—admiration.

80
Senility and Death

Apart from the demands made by religion, it may well be asked why it is more honorable in an aged man, who feels the decline of his powers, to await slow extinction than to fix a term to his existence himself? Suicide in such a case is a quite natural and due proceeding that ought to command respect as a triumph of reason: and did in fact command respect during the times of the masters of Greek philosophy and the bravest Roman patriots, who usually died by their own hand. Eagerness, on the other hand, to keep alive from day to day with the anxious counsel of physicians, without capacity to attain any nearer to one's ideal of life, is far less worthy of respect.—Religions are very rich in refuges from the mandate of suicide: hence they ingratiate themselves with those who cling to life.

FRIEDRICH NIETZSCHE

81
Delusions Regarding Victim and Regarding Evil Doer

When the rich man takes a possession away from the poor man (for example, a prince who deprives a plebeian of his beloved) there arises in the mind of the poor man a delusion: he thinks the rich man must be wholly perverted to take from him the little that he has. But the rich man appreciates the value of a single possession much less because he is accustomed to many possessions, so that he cannot put himself in the place of the poor man and does not act by any means as ill as the latter supposes. Both have a totally false idea of each other. The iniquities of the mighty which bulk most largely in history are not nearly so monstrous as they seem. The hereditary consciousness of being a superior being with superior environment renders one very callous and lulls the conscience to rest. We all feel, when the difference between ourselves and some other being is exceedingly great, that no element of injustice can be involved, and we kill a fly with no qualms of conscience whatever. So, too, it is no indication of wickedness in Xerxes (whom even the Greeks represent as exceptionally noble) that he deprived a father of his son and had him drawn and quartered because the latter had manifested a troublesome, ominous distrust of an entire expedition: the individual was in this case brushed aside as a pestiferous insect. He was too low and mean to justify continued sentiments of compunction in the ruler of the world. Indeed no cruel man is ever as cruel, in the main, as his victim thinks. The idea of pain is never the same as the sensation. The rule is precisely analogous in the case of the unjust judge, and of the journalist who by means of devious rhetorical methods, leads public opinion astray. Cause and effect are in all these instances entwined with totally different series of feeling and thoughts, whereas it is unconsciously assumed that principal and victim feel and think exactly alike, and because of this assumption the guilt of the one is based upon the pain of the other.

82
The Soul's Skin.

As the bones, flesh, entrails and blood vessels are enclosed by a skin that renders the aspect of men endurable, so the impulses and passions of the soul are enclosed by vanity: it is the skin of the soul.

83
Sleep of Virtue.

If virtue goes to sleep, it will be more vigorous when it awakes.

84
Subtlety of Shame.

Men are not ashamed of obscene thoughts, but they are ashamed when they suspect that obscene thoughts are attributed to them.

85
Naughtiness Is Rare.

Most people are too much absorbed in themselves to be bad.

86
The Mite in the Balance.

We are praised or blamed, as the one or the other may be expedient, for displaying to advantage our power of discernment.

87
Luke 18:14 Improved.

He that humbleth himself wisheth to be exalted.

88
Prevention of Suicide.

There is a justice according to which we may deprive a man of life, but none that permits us to deprive him of death: this is merely cruelty.

89
Vanity.

We set store by the good opinion of men, first because it is of use to us and next because we wish to give them pleasure (children their parents, pupils their teacher, and well disposed persons all others generally). Only when the good opinion of men is important to somebody, apart from personal advantage or the desire to give pleasure, do we speak of vanity. In this last case, a man wants to give himself pleasure, but at the expense of his fellow creatures, inasmuch as he inspires them with a false opinion of himself or else inspires "good opinion" in such a way that it is a source of pain to others (by arousing envy). The individual generally seeks, through the opinion of others, to attest and fortify the opinion he has of himself; but the potent influence of authority—an influence as old as man himself—leads many, also, to strengthen their own opinion of themselves by means of authority, that is, to borrow from others the expedient of relying more upon the judgment of their fellow men than upon their own.—Interest in oneself, the wish to please oneself attains, with the vain man, such proportions that he first misleads others into a false, unduly exalted estimate of himself and then relies upon the authority of others for his self estimate; he thus creates the delusion that he pins his faith to.—It must, however, be admitted that the vain man does not desire to please others so much as himself and he will often go so far, on this account, as to overlook his own interests: for he often inspires his fellow creatures with malicious envy and renders them ill disposed in order that he may thus increase his own delight in himself.

90
Limits of the Love of Mankind.

Every man who has declared that some other man is an ass or a scoundrel, gets angry when the other man conclusively shows that the assertion was erroneous.

91
Weeping Morality.

How much delight morality occasions! Think of the ocean of pleasing tears that has flowed from the narration of noble, great-hearted deeds!—This charm of life would disappear if the belief in complete irresponsibility gained the upper hand.

92
Origin of Justice.

Justice (reasonableness) has its origin among approximate equals in power, as Thucydides (in the dreadful conferences of the Athenian and Melian envoys) has rightly conceived. Thus, where there exists no demonstrable supremacy and a struggle leads but to mutual, useless damage, the reflection arises that an understanding would best be arrived at and some compromise entered into. The reciprocal nature is hence the first nature of justice. Each party makes the other content inasmuch as each receives what it prizes more highly than the other. Each surrenders to the other what the other wants and receives in return its own desire. Justice is therefore reprisal and exchange upon the basis of an approximate equality of power. Thus revenge pertains originally to the domain of justice as it is a sort of reciprocity. Equally so, gratitude.—Justice reverts naturally to the standpoint of self preservation, therefore to the egoism of this consideration: "why should I injure myself to no purpose and perhaps never attain my end?"—So much for the origin of justice. Only because men, through mental habits, have forgotten the original motive of so called just and rational acts, and also because for thousands of years children have been brought to admire and imitate such acts, have they gradually assumed the appearance of being unegotistical. Upon this appearance is founded the high estimate of them, which, moreover, like all estimates, is continually developing, for whatever is highly esteemed is striven for, imitated, made the object of self sacrifice, while the merit of the pain and emulation thus expended is, by each individual, ascribed to the thing esteemed.—How slightly moral would the world appear without forgetfulness! A poet could say that God had posted forgetfulness as a sentinel at the portal of the temple of human merit!

93
Concerning the Law of the Weaker.

Whenever any party, for instance, a besieged city, yields to a stronger party, under stipulated conditions, the counter stipulation is that there be a reduction to insignificance, a burning and destruction of the city and thus a great damage inflicted upon the stronger party. Thus arises a sort of equalization principle upon the basis of which a law can be established. The enemy has an advantage to gain by its maintenance. To this extent there is also a law between slaves and masters, limited only by the extent to which the slave may be useful to his master. The law goes originally only so far as the one party may appear to the other potent, invincible, stable, and the like. To such an extent, then, the weaker has rights, but very limited ones. Hence the famous dictum that each has as much law on his side as his power extends (or more accurately, as his power is believed to extend).

94
The Three Phases of Morality Hitherto.

It is the first evidence that the animal has become human

when his conduct ceases to be based upon the immediately expedient, but upon the permanently useful; when he has, therefore, grown utilitarian, capable of purpose. Thus is manifested the first rule of reason. A still higher stage is attained when he regulates his conduct upon the basis of honor, by means of which he gains mastery of himself and surrenders his desires to principles; this lifts him far above the phase in which he was actuated only by considerations of personal advantage as he understood it. He respects and wishes to be respected. This means that he comprehends utility as a thing dependent upon what his opinion of others is and their opinion of him. Finally he regulates his conduct (the highest phase of morality hitherto attained) by his own standard of men and things. He himself decides, for himself and for others, what is honorable and what is useful. He has become a law giver to opinion, upon the basis of his ever higher developing conception of the utilitarian and the honorable. Knowledge makes him capable of placing the highest utility, (that is, the universal, enduring utility) before merely personal utility,—of placing ennobling recognition of the enduring and universal before the merely temporary: he lives and acts as a collective individuality.

95
Ethic of the Developed Individual.

Hitherto the altruistic has been looked upon as the distinctive characteristic of moral conduct, and it is manifest that it was the consideration of universal utility that prompted praise and recognition of altruistic conduct. Must not a radical departure from this point of view be imminent, now that it is being ever more clearly perceived that in the most personal considerations the most general welfare is attained: so that conduct inspired by the most personal considerations of advantage is just the sort which has its origin in the present conception of morality (as a universal utilitarianism)? To contemplate oneself as a complete personality and bear the welfare of that personality in mind in all that one does—this is productive of better results than any sympathetic susceptibility and conduct in behalf of others. Indeed we all suffer from such disparagement of our own personalities, which are at present made to deteriorate from neglect. Capacity is, in fact, divorced from our personality in most cases, and sacrificed to the state, to science, to the needy, as if it were the bad which deserved to be made a sacrifice. Now, we are willing to labor for our fellowmen but only to the extent that we find our own highest advantage in so doing, no more, no less. The whole matter depends upon what may be understood as one's advantage: the crude, undeveloped, rough individualities will be the very ones to estimate it most inadequately.

96
Usage and Ethic.

To be moral, virtuous, praiseworthy means to yield obedience to ancient law and hereditary usage. Whether this obedience be rendered readily or with difficulty is long immaterial. Enough that it be rendered. "Good" finally comes to mean him who acts in the traditional manner, as a result of heredity or natural disposition, that is to say does what is customary with scarcely an effort, whatever that may be (for example revenges injuries when revenge, as with the ancient Greeks, was part of good morals). He is called good because he is good "to some purpose," and as benevolence, sympathy, considerateness, moderation and the like come, in the general course of conduct, to be finally recognized as "good to some purpose" (as utilitarian) the benevolent man, the helpful man, is duly styled "good". (At first other and more important kinds of utilitarian qualities stand in the foreground.) Bad is "not habitual" (unusual), to do things not in accordance with usage, to oppose the traditional, however rational or the reverse the traditional may be. To do injury to one's social group or community (and to one's neighbor as thus understood) is looked upon, through all the variations of moral laws, in different ages, as the peculiarly "immoral" act, so that to-day we associate the word "bad" with deliberate injury to one's neighbor or community. "Egoistic" and "non-egoistic" do not constitute the fundamental opposites that have brought mankind to make a distinction between moral and immoral, good and bad; but adherence to traditional custom, and emancipation from it. How the traditional had its origin is quite immaterial; in any event it had no reference to good and bad or any categorical imperative but to the all important end of maintaining and sustaining the community, the race, the confederation, the nation. Every superstitious custom that originated in a misinterpreted event or casualty entailed some tradition, to adhere to which is moral. To break loose from it is dangerous, more prejudicial to the community than to the individual (because divinity visits the consequences of impiety and sacrilege upon the community rather than upon the individual). Now every tradition grows ever more venerable—the more remote is its origin, the more confused that origin is. The reverence due to it increases from generation to generation. The tradition finally becomes holy and inspires awe. Thus it is that the precept of piety is a far loftier morality than that inculcated by altruistic conduct.

97
Delight in the Moral.

A potent species of joy (and thereby the source of morality) is custom. The customary is done more easily, better, therefore preferably. A pleasure is felt in it and experience thus shows that since this practice has held its own it must be good. A manner or moral that lives and lets live is thus demonstrated advantageous, necessary, in contradistinction to all new and not yet adopted practices. The custom is therefore the blending of the agreeable and the useful. Moreover it does not require deliberation. As soon as man can exercise compulsion, he exercises it to enforce and establish his customs, for they are to him attested lifewisdom. So, too, a community of individuals constrains each one of their number to adopt the same moral or custom. The error herein is this: Because a certain custom has been agreeable to the feelings or at least because it proves a means of maintenance, this custom must be imperative, for it is regarded as the only thing that can possibly be consistent with well being. The well being of life seems to spring from it alone. This conception of the customary as a condition of existence is carried into the slightest detail of morality. Inasmuch as insight into true causation is quite restricted in all inferior peoples, a superstitious anxiety is felt that everything be done in due routine. Even when a custom is exceedingly burdensome it is preserved because of its supposed vital utility. It is not known that the same degree of satisfaction can be experienced through some other custom and even higher degrees of satisfaction, too. But it is fully appreciated that all customs do become more agreeable with the lapse of time, no matter how difficult they may have been found in the beginning, and that even the severest way of life may be rendered a matter of habit and therefore a pleasure.

98
Pleasure and Social Instinct.

Through his relations with other men, man derives a new species of delight in those pleasurable emotions which his own personality affords him; whereby the domain of pleasurable emotions is made infinitely more comprehensive. No doubt he has inherited many of these feelings from the brutes, which palpably feel delight when they sport with one another, as mothers with their young. So, too, the sexual relations must be taken into account: they make every young woman interesting to every young man from the standpoint of pleasure, and conversely. The feeling of pleasure originating in human relationships makes men in general better. The delight in common, the pleasures enjoyed together heighten one another. The individual feels a sense of security. He becomes better natured. Distrust and malice dissolve. For the man feels the sense of benefit and observes the same feeling in others. Mutual manifestations of pleasure inspire mutual sympathy, the sentiment of homogeneity. The same effect is felt also at mutual sufferings, in a common danger, in stormy weather. Upon such a foundation are built the earliest alliances: the object of which is the mutual protection and safety from threatening misfortunes, and the welfare of each individual. And thus the social instinct develops from pleasure.

99
The Guiltless Nature of So-Called Bad Acts.

All "bad" acts are inspired by the impulse to self preservation or, more accurately, by the desire for pleasure and for the avoidance of pain in the individual. Thus are they occasioned, but they are not, therefore, bad. "Pain self prepared" does not exist, except in the brains of the philosophers, any more than "pleasure self prepared" (sympathy in the Schopenhauer sense). In the condition anterior to the state we kill the creature, be it man or ape, that attempts to pluck the fruit of a tree before we pluck it ourselves should we happen to be hungry at the time and making for that tree: as we would do to-day, so far as the brute is concerned, if we were wandering in savage regions.—The bad acts which most disturb us at present do so because of the erroneous supposition that the one who is guilty of them towards us has a free will in the matter and that it was within his discretion not to have done these evil things. This belief in discretionary power inspires hate, thirst for revenge, malice, the entire perversion of the mental processes, whereas we would feel in no way incensed against the brute, as we hold it irresponsible. To inflict pain not from the instinct of self preservation but in requital—this is the consequence of false judgment and is equally a guiltless course of conduct. The individual can, in that condition which is anterior to the state, act with fierceness and violence for the intimidation of another creature, in order to render his own power more secure as a result of such acts of intimidation. Thus acts the powerful, the superior, the original state founder, who subjugates the weaker. He has the right to do so, as the state nowadays assumes the same right, or, to be more accurate, there is no right that can conflict with this. A foundation for all morality can first be laid only when a stronger individuality or a collective individuality, for example society, the state, subjects the single personalities, hence builds upon their unification and establishes a bond of union. Morality results from compulsion, it is indeed itself one long compulsion to which obedience is rendered in order that pain may be avoided. At first it is but custom, later free obedience and finally almost instinct. At last it is (like everything habitual and natural) associated with pleasure—and is then called virtue.

100
Shame.

Shame exists wherever a "mystery" exists: but this is a religious notion which in the earlier period of human civilization had great vogue. Everywhere there were circumscribed spots to which access was denied on account of some divine law, except in special circumstances.

At first these spots were quite extensive, inasmuch as stipulated areas could not be trod by the uninitiated, who, when near them, felt tremors and anxieties. This sentiment was frequently transferred to other relationships, for example to sexual relations, which, as the privilege and gateway of mature age, must be withdrawn from the contemplation of youth for its own advantage: relations which many divinities were busy in preserving and sanctifying, images of which divinities were duly placed in marital chambers as guardians. (In Turkish such an apartment is termed a harem or holy thing, the same word also designating the vestibule of a mosque). So, too, Kingship is regarded as a centre from which power and brilliance stream forth, as a mystery to the subjects, impregnated with secrecy and shame, sentiments still quite operative among peoples who in other respects are without any shame at all. So, too, is the whole world of inward states, the so-called "soul," even now, for all non-philosophical persons, a "mystery," and during countless ages it was looked upon as a something of divine origin, in direct communion with deity. It is, therefore, an adytum and occasions shame.

101
Judge Not.

Care must be taken, in the contemplation of earlier ages, that there be no falling into unjust scornfulness. The injustice in slavery, the cruelty in the subjugation of persons and peoples must not be estimated by our standard. For in that period the instinct of justice was not so highly developed. Who dare reproach the Genoese Calvin for burning the physician Servetus at the stake? It was a proceeding growing out of his convictions. And the Inquisition, too, had its justification. The only thing is that the prevailing views were false and led to those proceedings which seem so cruel to us, simply because such views have become foreign to us. Besides, what is the burning alive of one individual compared with eternal hell pains for everybody else? And yet this idea then had hold of all the world without in the least vitiating, with its frightfulness, the other idea of a god. Even we nowadays are hard and merciless to political revolutionists, but that is because we are in the habit of believing the state a necessity, and hence the cruelty of the proceeding is not so much understood as in the other cases where the points of view are repudiated. The cruelty to animals shown by children and Italians is due to the same misunderstanding. The animal, owing to the exigencies of the church catechism, is placed too far below the level of mankind.—Much, too, that is frightful and inhuman in history, and which is almost incredible, is rendered less atrocious by the reflection that the one who commands and the one who executes are different persons. The former does not witness the performance and hence it makes no strong impression on him. The latter obeys a superior and hence feels no responsibility. Most princes and military chieftains appear, through lack of true perception, cruel and hard without really being so.—Egoism is not bad because the idea of the "neighbor"—the word is of Christian origin and does not correspond to truth—is very weak in us, and we feel ourselves, in regard to him, as free from responsibility as if plants and stones were involved. That another is in suffering must be learned and it can never be wholly learned.

102
"Man Always Does Right."

We do not blame nature when she sends a thunder storm and makes us wet: why then do we term the man who inflicts injury immoral? Because in the latter case we assume a voluntary, ruling, free will, and in the former necessity. But this distinction is a delusion. Moreover, even the intentional infliction of injury is not, in all circumstances termed immoral. Thus, we kill a fly intentionally without thinking very much about it, simply because its buzzing about is disagreeable; and we punish a criminal and inflict pain upon him in order to protect ourselves and society. In the first case it is the individual who, for the sake of preserving himself or in order to spare himself pain, does injury with design: in the second case, it is the state. All ethic deems intentional infliction of injury justified by necessity; that is when it is a matter of self preservation. But these two points of view are sufficient to explain all bad acts done by man to men. It is desired to obtain pleasure or avoid pain. In any sense, it is a question, always, of self preservation. Socrates and Plato are right: whatever man does he always does right: that is, does what seems to him good (advantageous) according to the degree of advancement his intellect has attained, which is always the measure of his rational capacity.

103
The Inoffensive in Badness.

Badness has not for its object the infliction of pain upon others but simply our own satisfaction as, for instance, in the case of thirst for vengeance or of nerve excitation. Every act of teasing shows what pleasure is caused by the display of our power over others and what feelings of delight are experienced in the sense of domination. Is there, then, anything immoral in feeling pleasure in the pain of others? Is malicious joy devilish, as Schopenhauer says? In the realm of nature we feel joy in breaking boughs, shattering rocks, fighting with wild beasts, simply to attest our strength thereby. Should not the knowledge that another suffers on our account here, in this case, make the same kind of act, (which, by the way, arouses no qualms of conscience in us) immoral also? But if we had not this knowledge there would be no pleasure in one's own superiority or power, for this pleasure is experienced only in the suffering of another, as in the case of teasing. All pleasure is, in itself, neither good nor bad. Whence comes the conviction that one should not cause pain in others in order to feel pleasure oneself? Simply from the standpoint of utility, that is, in consideration of the consequences, of ultimate pain, since the injured party or state will demand satisfaction and revenge. This consideration alone can have led to the determination to renounce such pleasure.—Sympathy has the satisfaction of others in view no more than, as already stated, badness has the pain of others in view. For there are at least two (perhaps many more) elementary ingredients in personal gratification which enter largely into our self satisfaction: one of them being the pleasure of the emotion, of which species is sympathy with tragedy, and another, when the impulse is to action, being the pleasure of exercising one's power. Should a sufferer be very dear to us, we divest ourselves of pain by the performance of acts of sympathy.—With the exception of some few philosophers, men have placed sympathy very low in the rank of moral feelings: and rightly.

104
Self Defence.

If self defence is in general held a valid justification, then nearly every manifestation of so called immoral egoism must be justified, too. Pain is inflicted, robbery or killing done in order to maintain life or to protect oneself and ward off harm. A man lies when cunning and delusion are valid means of self preservation. To injure intentionally when our safety and our existence are

involved, or the continuance of our well being, is co
moral. The state itself injures from this motive wh...
criminals. In unintentional injury the immoral, of course, can n...
be present, as accident alone is involved. But is there any sort of
intentional injury in which our existence and the maintenance of
our well being be not involved?

Is there such a thing as injuring from absolute badness, for
example, in the case of cruelty? If a man does not know what
pain an act occasions, that act is not one of wickedness. Thus the
child is not bad to the animal, not evil. It disturbs and rends it as
if it were one of its playthings. Does a man ever fully know how
much pain an act may cause another? As far as our nervous
system extends, we shield ourselves from pain. If it extended
further, that is, to our fellow men, we would never cause anyone
else any pain (except in such cases as we cause it to ourselves,
when we cut ourselves, surgically, to heal our ills, or strive and
trouble ourselves to gain health). We conclude from analogy that
something pains somebody and can in consequence, through
recollection and the power of imagination, feel pain also. But
what a difference there always is between the tooth ache and the
pain (sympathy) that the spectacle of tooth ache occasions!
Therefore when injury is inflicted from so called badness the
degree of pain thereby experienced is always unknown to us: in
so far, however, as pleasure is felt in the act (a sense of one's own
power, of one's own excitation) the act is committed to maintain
the well being of the individual and hence comes under the
purview of self defence and lying for self preservation. Without
pleasure, there is no life; the struggle for pleasure is the struggle
for life. Whether the individual shall carry on this struggle in such
a way that he be called good or in such a way that he be called
bad is something that the standard and the capacity of his own
intellect must determine for him.

105
Justice that Rewards.

Whoever has fully understood the doctrine of absolute

irresponsibility can no longer include the so called rewarding and punishing justice in the idea of justice, if the latter be taken to mean that to each be given his due. For he who is punished does not deserve the punishment. He is used simply as a means to intimidate others from certain acts. Equally, he who is rewarded does not merit the reward. He could not act any differently than he did act. Hence the reward has only the significance of an encouragement to him and others as a motive for subsequent acts. The praise is called out only to him who is running in the race and not to him who has arrived at the goal. Something that comes to someone as his own is neither a punishment nor a reward. It is given to him from utiliarian considerations, without his having any claim to it in justice. Hence one must say "the wise man praises not because a good act has been done" precisely as was once said: "the wise man punishes not because a bad act has been done but in order that a bad act may not be done." If punishment and reward ceased, there would cease with them the most powerful incentives to certain acts and away from other acts. The purposes of men demand their continuance [of punishment and reward] and inasmuch as punishment and reward, blame and praise operate most potently upon vanity, these same purposes of men imperatively require the continuance of vanity.

106
The Water Fall.

At the sight of a water fall we may opine that in the countless curves, spirations and dashes of the waves we behold freedom of the will and of the impulses. But everything is compulsory, everything can be mathematically calculated. Thus it is, too, with human acts. We would be able to calculate in advance every single action if we were all knowing, as well as every advance in knowledge, every delusion, every bad deed. The acting individual himself is held fast in the illusion of volition. If, on a sudden, the entire movement of the world stopped short, and an all knowing and reasoning intelligence were there to take advantage of this pause, he could foretell the future of every being to the remotest ages and indicate the path that would be taken in the world's further course. The deception of the acting individual as regards himself, the assumption of the freedom of the will, is a part of this computable mechanism.

107
Non-Responsibility and Non-Guilt.

The absolute irresponsibility of man for his acts and his nature is the bitterest drop in the cup of him who has knowledge, if he be accustomed to behold in responsibility and duty the patent of nobility of his human nature. All his estimates, preferences, dislikes are thus made worthless and false. His deepest sentiment, with which he honored the sufferer, the hero, sprang from an error. He may no longer praise, no longer blame, for it is irrational to blame and praise nature and necessity. Just as he cherishes the beautiful work of art, but does not praise it (as it is incapable of doing anything for itself), just as he stands in the presence of plants, he must stand in the presence of human conduct, his own included. He may admire strength, beauty, capacity, therein, but he can discern no merit. The chemical process and the conflict of the elements, the ordeal of the invalid who strives for convalescence, are no more merits than the soul-struggles and extremities in which one is torn this way and that by contending motives until one finally decides in favor of the strongest—as the phrase has it, although, in fact, it is the strongest motive that decides for us. All these motives, however, whatever fine names we may give them, have grown from the same roots in which we believe the baneful poisons lurk. Between good and bad actions there is no difference in kind but, at most, in degree. Good acts are sublimated evil. Bad acts are degraded, imbruted good. The very longing of the individual for self gratification (together with the fear of being deprived of it) obtains satisfaction in all circumstances, let the individual act as he may, that is, as he must: be it in deeds of vanity, revenge, pleasure, utility, badness, cunning, be it in deeds of self sacrifice, sympathy or knowledge. The degrees of rational capacity determine the direction in which this longing impels: every society, every individual has constantly present a comparative classification of benefits in accordance with which conduct is determined and others are judged. But this standard perpetually changes. Many acts are called bad that are only stupid, because the degree of intelligence that decided for them was low. Indeed, in a certain sense, all acts now are stupid, for the highest degree of human intelligence that has yet been attained will in time most certainly be surpassed and then, in retrospection, all our present conduct and opinion will appear as narrow and petty as we now deem the conduct and opinion of savage peoples and ages.—To perceive all these things may occasion profound pain but there is, nevertheless, a consolation. Such pains are birth pains. The butterfly insists upon breaking through the cocoon, he presses through it, tears it to pieces, only to be blinded and confused by the strange light, by the realm of liberty. By such men as are capable of this sadness—how few there are!—will the first attempt be made to see if humanity may convert itself from a thing of morality to a thing of wisdom. The sun of a new gospel sheds its first ray upon the loftiest height in the souls of those few: but the clouds are massed there, too, thicker than ever, and not far apart are the brightest sunlight and the deepest gloom. Everything is necessity—so says the new knowledge: and this knowledge is itself necessity. All is guiltlessness, and knowledge is the way to insight into this guiltlessness. If pleasure, egoism, vanity be necessary to attest the moral phenomena and their richest blooms, the instinct for truth and accuracy of knowledge; if delusion and confusion of the imagination were the only means whereby mankind could gradually lift itself up to this degree of self enlightenment and self emancipation—who would venture to disparage the means? Who would have the right to feel sad if made aware of the goal to which those paths lead? Everything in the domain of ethic is evolved, changeable, tottering; all things flow, it is true—but all things are also in the stream: to their goal. Though within us the hereditary habit of erroneous judgment, love, hate, may be ever dominant, yet under

FRIEDRICH NIETZSCHE

the influence of awaking knowledge it will ever become weaker: a new habit, that of understanding, not-loving, not-hating, looking from above, grows up within us gradually and in the same soil, and may, perhaps, in thousands of years be powerful enough to endow mankind with capacity to develop the wise, guiltless man (conscious of guiltlessness) as unfailingly as it now developes the unwise, irrational, guilt-conscious man—that is to say, the necessary higher step, not the opposite of it.

THE RELIGIOUS LIFE.

108
The Double Contest Against Evil.

If an evil afflicts us we can either so deal with it as to remove its cause or else so deal with it that its effect upon our feeling is changed: hence look upon the evil as a benefit of which the uses will perhaps first become evident in some subsequent period. Religion and art (and also the metaphysical philosophy) strive to effect an alteration of the feeling, partly by an alteration of our judgment respecting the experience (for example, with the aid of the dictum "whom God loves, he chastizes") partly by the awakening of a joy in pain, in emotion especially (whence the art of tragedy had its origin). The more one is disposed to interpret away and justify, the less likely he is to look directly at the causes of evil and eliminate them. An instant alleviation and narcotizing of pain, as is usual in the case of tooth ache, is sufficient for him even in the severest suffering. The more the domination of religions and of all narcotic arts declines, the more searchingly do men look to the elimination of evil itself, which is a rather bad thing for the tragic poets—for there is ever less and less material for tragedy, since the domain of unsparing, immutable destiny grows constantly more circumscribed, and a still worse thing for the priests, for these last have lived heretofore upon the narcoticizing of human ill.

109
Sorrow is Knowledge.

How willingly would not one exchange the false assertions of the homines religiosi that there is a god who commands us to be good, who is the sentinel and witness of every act, every moment, every thought, who loves us, who plans our welfare in every misfortune—how willingly would not one exchange these for truths as healing, beneficial and grateful as those delusions! But there are no such truths. Philosophy can at most set up in opposition to them other metaphysical plausibilities (fundamental untruths as well). The tragedy of it all is that, although one cannot believe these dogmas of religion and metaphysics if one adopts in heart and head the potent methods of truth, one has yet become, through human evolution, so tender, susceptible, sensitive, as to stand in need of the most effective means of rest and consolation. From this state of things arises the danger that, through the perception of truth or, more accurately, seeing through delusion, one may bleed to death. Byron has put this into deathless verse:

> "Sorrow is knowledge: they who know the most
> Must mourn the deepest o'er the fatal truth,
> The tree of knowledge is not that of life."

Against such cares there is no better protective than the light fancy of Horace, (at any rate during the darkest hours and sun eclipses of the soul) expressed in the words

"quid aeternis minorem
consiliis animum fatigas?
cur non sub alta vel platano vel hac
pinu jacentes."*

---

* *Then wherefore should you, who are mortal, outwear*

At any rate, light fancy or heavy heartedness of any degree must be better than a romantic retrogression and desertion of one's flag, an approach to Christianity in any form: for with it, in the present state of knowledge, one can have nothing to do without hopelessly defiling one's intellectual integrity and surrendering it unconditionally. These woes may be painful enough, but without pain one cannot become a leader and guide of humanity: and woe to him who would be such and lacks this pure integrity of the intellect!

110
The Truth in Religion.

In the ages of enlightenment justice was not done to the importance of religion, of this there can be no doubt. It is also equally certain that in the ensuing reaction of enlightenment, the demands of justice were far exceeded inasmuch as religion was treated with love, even with infatuation and proclaimed as a profound, indeed the most profound knowledge of the world, which science had but to divest of its dogmatic garb in order to possess "truth" in its unmythical form. Religions must therefore—this was the contention of all foes of enlightenment—sensu allegorico, with regard for the comprehension of the masses, give expression to that ancient truth which is wisdom in itself, inasmuch as all science of modern times has led up to it instead of away from it. So that between the most ancient wisdom of man and all later wisdom there prevails harmony, even similarity of viewpoint; and the advancement of knowledge—if one be disposed to concede such

---

Your soul with a profitless burden of care
Say, why should we not, flung at ease neath this pine,
Or a plane-tree's broad umbrage, quaff gaily our wine?
(Translation of Sir Theodore Martin.)

a thing—has to do not with its nature but with its propagation. This whole conception of religion and science is through and through erroneous, and none would to-day be hardy enough to countenance it had not Schopenhauer's rhetoric taken it under protection, this high sounding rhetoric which now gains auditors after the lapse of a generation. Much as may be gained from Schopenhauer's religio-ethical human and cosmical oracle as regards the comprehension of Christianity and other religions, it is nevertheless certain that he erred regarding the value of religion to knowledge. He himself was in this but a servile pupil of the scientific teachers of his time who had all taken romanticism under their protection and renounced the spirit of enlightenment. Had he been born in our own time it would have been impossible for him to have spoken of the sensus allegoricus of religion. He would instead have done truth the justice to say: never has a religion, directly or indirectly, either as dogma or as allegory, contained a truth. For all religions grew out of dread or necessity, and came into existence through an error of the reason. They have, perhaps, in times of danger from science, incorporated some philosophical doctrine or other into their systems in order to make it possible to continue one's existence within them. But this is but a theological work of art dating from the time in which a religion began to doubt of itself. These theological feats of art, which are most common in Christianity as the religion of a learned age, impregnated with philosophy, have led to this superstition of the sensus allegoricus, as has, even more, the habit of the philosophers (namely those half-natures, the poetical philosophers and the philosophising artists) of dealing with their own feelings as if they constituted the fundamental nature of humanity and hence of giving their own religious feelings a predominant influence over the structure of their systems. As the philosophers mostly philosophised under the influence of hereditary religious habits, or at least under the traditional influence of this "metaphysical necessity," they naturally arrived at conclusions closely resembling the Judaic or Christian or Indian religious tenets—resembling, in the way that children are apt to look like their mothers: only in this case the fathers were not certain as to the maternity, as easily happens—but in the innocence of their admiration, they fabled regarding the family likeness of all religion and science. In reality, there exists between religion and true science neither relationship nor friendship, not even enmity: they dwell in different spheres. Every philosophy that lets the religious comet gleam through the darkness of its last outposts renders everything within it that purports to be science, suspicious. It is all probably religion, although it may assume the guise of science.—Moreover, though all the peoples agree concerning certain religious things, for example, the existence of a god (which, by the way, as regards this point, is not the case) this fact would constitute an argument against the thing agreed upon, for example the very existence of a god. The consensus gentium and especially hominum can probably amount only to an absurdity. Against it there is no consensus omnium sapientium whatever, on any point, with the exception of which Goethe's verse speaks:

"All greatest sages to all latest ages
Will smile, wink and slily agree
'Tis folly to wait till a fool's empty pate
Has learned to be knowing and free.
So children of wisdom must look upon fools
As creatures who're never the better for schools."

Stated without rhyme or metre and adapted to our case: the consensus sapientium is to the effect that the consensus gentium amounts to an absurdity.

111
Origin of Religious Worship.

Let us transport ourselves back to the times in which religious life flourished most vigorously and we will find a fundamental conviction prevalent which we no longer share and which has resulted in the closing of the door to religious life once for all so far as we are concerned. This conviction has to do with nature and intercourse with her. In those times nothing is yet known of nature's laws. Neither for earth nor for heaven is there a must. A season, sunshine, rain can come or stay away as it pleases. There is wanting, in particular, all idea of natural causation. If a man rows, it is not the oar that moves the boat, but rowing is a magical ceremony whereby a demon is constrained to move the boat. All illness, death itself, is a consequence of magical influences. In sickness and death nothing natural is conceived. The whole idea of "natural course" is wanting. The idea dawns first upon the ancient Greeks, that is to say in a very late period of humanity, in the conception of a Moira [fate] ruling over the gods. If any person shoots off a bow, there is always an irrational strength and agency in the act. If the wells suddenly run dry, the first thought is of subterranean demons and their pranks. It must have been the dart of a god beneath whose invisible influence a human being suddenly collapses. In India, the carpenter (according to Lubbock) is in the habit of making devout offerings to his hammer and hatchet. A Brahmin treats the plume with which he writes, a soldier the weapon that he takes into the field, a mason his trowel, a laborer his plow, in the same way. All nature is, in the opinion of religious people, a sum total of the doings of conscious and willing beings, an immense mass of complex volitions. In regard to all that takes place outside of us no conclusion is permissible that anything will result thus and so, must result thus and so, that we are comparatively calculable and certain in our experiences, that man is the rule, nature the ruleless. This view forms the fundamental conviction that dominates crude, religion-producing, early civilizations. We contemporary men feel exactly the opposite: the richer man now feels himself inwardly, the more polyphone the music and the sounding of his soul, the more powerfully does the uniformity of nature impress him. We all, with Goethe, recognize in nature the great means of repose for the soul. We listen to the pendulum stroke of this great clock with longing for rest, for absolute calm and quiescence, as if we could drink in the uniformity of nature and thereby arrive first at an enjoyment of oneself. Formerly it was the reverse: if we carry ourselves back to the periods of crude civilization, or if we contemplate contemporary savages, we will find them most strongly influenced by rule, by tradition. The individual is almost automatically bound to rule and tradition and moves with the uniformity of a pendulum. To him nature—the uncomprehended, fearful, mysterious nature—must seem the domain of freedom, of volition, of higher power, indeed as an ultra-human degree of destiny, as god. Every individual in such periods and circumstances feels that his existence, his happiness, the existence and happiness of the family, the state, the success or failure of every undertaking, must depend upon these dispositions of nature. Certain natural events must occur at the proper time and certain others must not occur. How can influence be exercised over this fearful unknown, how can this domain of freedom be brought under subjection? thus he asks himself, thus he worries: Is there no means to render these powers of nature as subject to rule and tradition as you are yourself?—The cogitation of the superstitious and magic-deluded man is upon the theme of imposing a law upon nature: and to put it briefly, religious worship is the result of such cogitation. The problem which is present to every man is closely connected with this one: how can the weaker party dictate laws to the stronger, control its acts in reference to the weaker? At first the most harmless form of influence is recollected, that influence which is acquired when the partiality of anyone has been won. Through beseeching and prayer, through abject humiliation, through obligations to regular gifts and propitiations, through flattering homages, it is possible, therefore, to impose some guidance upon the forces of nature, to the extent that their partiality be won: love binds and is bound. Then agreements can be entered into by means of which certain courses of conduct are mutually concluded, vows are made and authorities prescribed. But far more potent is that species of power exercised by means of magic and incantation. As a man is able to injure a powerful enemy by means of the magician and render him helpless with fear, as the love potion operates at a distance, so can the mighty forces of nature, in the opinion of weaker mankind, be controlled by similar means. The principal means of effecting incantations is to acquire control of something belonging to the party to be influenced, hair, finger nails, food from his table, even his picture or his name. With such apparatus it is possible to act by means of magic, for the basic principle is that to everything spiritual corresponds something corporeal. With the aid of this corporeal element the spirit may be bound, injured or destroyed. The corporeal affords the handle by which the spiritual can be laid hold of. In the same way that man influences mankind does he influences some spirit of nature, for this latter has also its corporeal element that can be grasped. The tree, and on the same basis, the seed from which it grew: this puzzling sequence seems to demonstrate that in both forms the same spirit is embodied, now large, now small. A stone that suddenly rolls, is the body in which the spirit works. Does a huge boulder lie in lonely moor? It is impossible to think of mortal power having placed it there. The stone must have moved itself there. That is to say some spirit must dominate it. Everything that has a body is subject to magic, including, therefore, the spirits of nature. If a god is directly connected with his portrait, a direct influence (by refraining from devout offerings, by whippings, chainings and the like) can be brought to bear upon him. The lower classes in China tie cords around the picture of their god in order to defy his departing favor, when he has left them in the lurch, and tear the picture to pieces, drag it through the streets into dung heaps and gutters, crying: "You dog of a spirit, we housed you in a beautiful temple, we gilded you prettily, we fed you well, we brought you offerings, and yet how ungrateful you are!" Similar displays of resentment have been made against pictures of the mother of god and pictures of saints in Catholic countries during the present century when such pictures would not do their duty during times of pestilence and drought.

Through all these magical relationships to nature countless ceremonies are occasioned, and finally, when their complexity and confusion grow too great, pains are taken to systematize them, to arrange them so that the favorable course of nature's progress, namely the great yearly circle of the seasons, may be brought about by a corresponding course of the ceremonial progress. The aim of religious worship is to influence nature to human advantage, and hence to instil a subjection to law into her that originally she has not, whereas at present man desires to find out the subjection to law of nature in order to guide himself thereby. In brief, the system of religious worship rests upon the idea of magic between man and man, and the magician is older than the priest. But it rests equally upon other and higher ideas. It brings into prominence the sympathetic relation of man to man, the existence of benevolence, gratitude, prayer, of truces between enemies, of loans upon security, of arrangements for the protection of property. Man, even in very inferior degrees of civilization, does not stand in the presence of nature as a helpless slave, he is not willy-nilly the absolute servant of nature. In the Greek development of religion, especially in the relationship to the Olympian gods, it becomes possible to entertain the idea of an existence side by side of two castes, a higher, more powerful, and a lower, less powerful: but both are bound together in some way, on account of their origin and are one species. They need not be ashamed of one another. This is the element of distinction in Greek religion.

112
At the Contemplation of Certain Ancient Sacrificial Proceedings.

How many sentiments are lost to us is manifest in the union of the farcical, even of the obscene, with the religious feeling. The feeling that this mixture is possible is becoming extinct. We realize the mixture only historically, in the mysteries of Demeter and Dionysos and in the Christian Easter festivals and religious mysteries. But we still perceive the sublime in connection with the ridiculous, and the like, the emotional with the absurd. Perhaps a later age will be unable to understand even these combinations.

113
Christianity as Antiquity.

When on a Sunday morning we hear the old bells ringing, we ask ourselves: Is it possible? All this for a Jew crucified two thousand years ago who said he was God's son? The proof of such an assertion is lacking.—Certainly, the Christian religion constitutes in our time a protruding bit of antiquity from very remote ages and that its assertions are still generally believed—although men have become so keen in the scrutiny of claims—constitutes the oldest relic of this inheritance. A god who begets children by a mortal woman; a sage who demands that no more work be done, that no more justice be administered but that the signs of the approaching end of the world be heeded; a system of justice that accepts an innocent as a vicarious sacrifice in the place of the guilty; a person who bids his disciples drink his blood; prayers for miracles; sins against a god expiated upon a god; fear of a hereafter to which death is the portal; the figure of the cross as a symbol in an age that no longer knows the purpose and the ignominy of the cross—how ghostly all these things flit before us out of the grave of their primitive antiquity! Is one to believe that such things can still be believed?

114
The Un-Greek in Christianity.

The Greeks did not look upon the Homeric gods above them as lords nor upon themselves beneath as servants, after the fashion of the Jews. They saw but the counterpart as in a mirror of the most perfect specimens of their own caste, hence an ideal, but no contradiction of their own nature. There was a feeling of mutual relationship, resulting in a mutual interest, a sort of alliance. Man thinks well of himself when he gives himself such gods and places himself in a relationship akin to that of the lower nobility with the higher; whereas the Italian races have a decidedly vulgar religion, involving perpetual anxiety because of bad and mischievous powers and soul disturbers. Wherever the Olympian gods receded into the background, there even Greek life became gloomier and more perturbed.—Christianity, on the other hand, oppressed and degraded humanity completely and sank it into deepest mire: into the feeling of utter abasement it suddenly flashed the gleam of divine compassion, so that the amazed and grace-dazzled stupefied one gave a cry of delight and for a moment believed that the whole of heaven was within him. Upon this unhealthy excess of feeling, upon the accompanying corruption of heart and head, Christianity attains all its psychological effects. It wants to annihilate, debase, stupefy, amaze, bedazzle. There is but one thing that it does not want: measure, standard (das Maas) and therefore is it in the worst sense barbarous, asiatic, vulgar, un-Greek.

115
Being Religious to Some Purpose.

There are certain insipid, traffic-virtuous people to whom religion is pinned like the hem of some garb of a higher humanity. These people do well to remain religious: it adorns them. All who are not versed in some professional weapon—including tongue and pen as weapons—are servile: to all such the Christian religion is very useful, for then their servility assumes the aspect of Christian virtue and is amazingly adorned.—People whose daily lives are empty and colorless are readily religious. This is comprehensible and pardonable, but they have no right to demand that others, whose daily lives are not empty and colorless, should be religious also.

116
The Everyday Christian.

If Christianity, with its allegations of an avenging God, universal sinfulness, choice of grace, and the danger of eternal damnation, were true, it would be an indication of weakness of mind and character not to be a priest or an apostle or a hermit, and toil for one's own salvation. It would be irrational to lose sight of one's eternal well being in comparison with temporary advantage: Assuming these dogmas to be generally believed, the every day Christian is a pitiable figure, a man who really cannot count as far as three, and who, for the rest, just because of his intellectual incapacity, does not deserve to be as hard punished as Christianity promises he shall be.

117
Concerning the Cleverness of Christianity.

It is a master stroke of Christianity to so emphasize the unworthiness, sinfulness and degradation of men in general that contempt of one's fellow creatures becomes impossible. "He may sin as much as he pleases, he is not by nature different from me. It is I who in every way am unworthy and contemptible." So says the Christian to himself. But even this feeling has lost its keenest sting for the Christian does not believe in his individual degradation. He is bad in his general human capacity and he soothes himself a little with the assertion that we are all alike.

118
Personal Change.

As soon as a religion rules, it has for its opponents those who were its first disciples.

119
Fate of Christianity.

Christianity arose to lighten the heart, but now it must first make the heart heavy in order to be able to lighten it afterwards. Christianity will consequently go down.

120
The Testimony of Pleasure.

The agreeable opinion is accepted as true. This is the testimony of pleasure (or as the church says, the evidence of strength) of which all religions are so proud, although they should all be ashamed of it. If a belief did not make blessed it would not be believed. How little it would be worth, then!

121
Dangerous Play.

Whoever gives religious feeling room, must then also let it grow. He can do nothing else. Then his being gradually changes. The religious element brings with it affinities and kinships. The whole circle of his judgment and feeling is clouded and draped in religious shadows. Feeling cannot stand still. One should be on one's guard.

122
The Blind Pupil.

As long as one knows very well the strength and the weakness of one's dogma, one's art, one's religion, its strength is still low. The pupil and apostle who has no eye for the weaknesses of a dogma, a religion and so on, dazzled by the aspect of the master and by his own reverence for him, has, on that very account, generally more power than the master. Without blind pupils the influence of a man and his work has never become great. To give victory to knowledge, often amounts to no more than so allying it with stupidity that the brute force of the latter forces triumph for the former.

123
The Breaking off of Churches.

There is not sufficient religion in the world merely to put an end to the number of religions.

124
Sinlessness of Men.

If one have understood how "Sin came into the world," namely through errors of the reason, through which men in their intercourse with one another and even individual men looked upon themselves as much blacker and wickeder than was really the case, one's whole feeling is much lightened and man and the world appear together in such a halo of harmlessness that a sentiment of well being is instilled into one's whole nature. Man in the midst of nature is as a child left to its own devices. This child indeed dreams a heavy, anxious dream. But when it opens its eyes it finds itself always in paradise.

125
Irreligiousness of Artists.

Homer is so much at home among his gods and is as a poet so good natured to them that he must have been profoundly irreligious. That which was brought to him by the popular faith—a mean, crude and partially repulsive superstition—he dealt with as freely as the Sculptor with his clay, therefore with the same freedom that Æschylus and Aristophanes evinced and with which in later times the great artists of the renaissance, and also Shakespeare and Goethe, drew their pictures.

126
Art and Strength of False Interpretation.

All the visions, fears, exhaustions and delights of the saint are well known symptoms of sickness, which in him, owing to deep rooted religious and psychological delusions, are explained quite differently, that is not as symptoms of sickness.—So, too, perhaps, the demon of Socrates was nothing but a malady of the ear that he explained, in view of his predominant moral theory, in a manner different from what would be thought rational today. Nor is the case different with the frenzy and the frenzied speeches of the prophets and of the priests of the oracles. It is always the degree of wisdom, imagination, capacity and morality in the heart and mind of the interpreters that got so much out of them. It is among the greatest feats of the men who are called geniuses and saints that they made interpreters for themselves who, fortunately for mankind, did not understand them.

127
Reverence for Madness.

Because it was perceived that an excitement of some kind often made the head clearer and occasioned fortunate inspirations, it was concluded that the utmost excitement would occasion the most fortunate inspirations. Hence the frenzied being was revered as a sage and an oracle giver. A false conclusion lies at the bottom of all this.

128
Promises of Wisdom.

Modern science has as its object as little pain as possible, as long a life as possible—hence a sort of eternal blessedness, but of a very limited kind in comparison with the promises of religion.

129
Forbidden Generosity.

There is not enough of love and goodness in the world to throw any of it away on conceited people.

130
Survival of Religious Training in the Disposition.

The Catholic Church, and before it all ancient education,

controlled the whole domain of means through which man was put into certain unordinary moods and withdrawn from the cold calculation of personal advantage and from calm, rational reflection. A church vibrating with deep tones; gloomy, regular, restraining exhortations from a priestly band, who involuntarily communicate their own tension to their congregation and lead them to listen almost with anxiety as if some miracle were in course of preparation; the awesome pile of architecture which, as the house of a god, rears itself vastly into the vague and in all its shadowy nooks inspires fear of its nerve-exciting power—who would care to reduce men to the level of these things if the ideas upon which they rest became extinct? But the results of all these things are nevertheless not thrown away: the inner world of exalted, emotional, prophetic, profoundly repentant, hope-blessed moods has become inborn in man largely through cultivation. What still exists in his soul was formerly, as he germinated, grew and bloomed, thoroughly disciplined.

131
Religious After-Pains.

Though one believe oneself absolutely weaned away from religion, the process has yet not been so thorough as to make impossible a feeling of joy at the presence of religious feelings and dispositions without intelligible content, as, for example, in music; and if a philosophy alleges to us the validity of metaphysical hopes, through the peace of soul therein attainable, and also speaks of "the whole true gospel in the look of Raphael's Madonna," we greet such declarations and innuendoes with a welcome smile. The philosopher has here a matter easy of demonstration. He responds with that which he is glad to give, namely a heart that is glad to accept. Hence it is observable how the less reflective free spirits collide only with dogmas but yield readily to the magic of religious feelings; it is a source of pain to them to let the latter go simply on account of the former.—Scientific philosophy must be very much on its guard lest on account of this necessity—an evolved and hence, also, a transitory necessity—delusions are smuggled in. Even logicians speak of "presentiments" of truth in ethics and in art (for example of the presentiment that the essence of things is unity) a thing which, nevertheless, ought to be prohibited. Between carefully deduced truths and such "foreboded" things there lies the abysmal distinction that the former are products of the intellect and the latter of the necessity.

Hunger is no evidence that there is food at hand to appease it. Hunger merely craves food. "Presentiment" does not denote that the existence of a thing is known in any way whatever. It denotes merely that it is deemed possible to the extent that it is desired or feared. The "presentiment" is not one step forward in the domain of certainty.—It is involuntarily believed that the religious tinted sections of a philosophy are better attested than the others, but the case is at bottom just the opposite: there is simply the inner wish that it may be so, that the thing which beautifies may also be true. This wish leads us to accept bad grounds as good.

132
Of the Christian Need of Salvation.

Careful consideration must render it possible to propound some explanation of that process in the soul of a Christian which is termed need of salvation, and to propound an explanation, too, free from mythology: hence one purely psychological. Heretofore psychological explanations of religious conditions and processes have really been in disrepute, inasmuch as a theology calling itself free gave vent to its unprofitable nature in this domain; for its principal aim, so far as may be judged from the spirit of its creator, Schleier-macher, was the preservation of the Christian religion and the maintenance of the Christian theology. It appeared that in the psychological analysis of religious "facts" a new anchorage and above all a new calling were to be gained. Undisturbed by such predecessors, we venture the following exposition of the phenomena alluded to. Man is conscious of certain acts which are very firmly implanted in the general course of conduct: indeed he discovers in himself a predisposition to such acts that seems to him to be as unalterable as his very being. How gladly he would essay some other kind of acts which in the general estimate of conduct are rated the best and highest, how gladly he would welcome the consciousness of well doing which ought to follow unselfish motive! Unfortunately, however, it goes no further than this longing: the discontent consequent upon being unable to satisfy it is added to all other kinds of discontent which result from his life destiny in particular or which may be due to so called bad acts; so that a deep depression ensues accompanied by a desire for some physician to remove it and all its causes.—This condition would not be found so bitter if the individual but compared himself freely with other men: for then he would have no reason to be discontented with himself in particular as he is merely bearing his share of the general burden of human discontent and incompleteness. But he compares himself with a being who alone must be capable of the conduct that is called unegoistic and of an enduring consciousness of unselfish motive, with God. It is because he gazes into this clear mirror, that his own self seems so extraordinarily distracted and so troubled. Thereupon the thought of that being, in so far as it flits before his fancy as retributive justice, occasions him anxiety. In every conceivable small and great experience he believes he sees the anger of the being, his threats, the very implements and manacles of his judge and prison. What succors him in this danger, which, in the prospect of an eternal duration of punishment, transcends in hideousness all the horrors that can be presented to the imagination?

133

Before we consider this condition in its further effects, we would admit to ourselves that man is betrayed into this condition not through his "fault" and "sin" but through a series of delusions of the reason; that it was the fault of the mirror if his own self appeared to him in the highest degree dark and hateful, and that that mirror was his own work, the very imperfect work of human imagination and judgment. In the first place a being capable of absolutely unegoistic conduct is as fabulous as the phoenix. Such a being is not even thinkable for the very reason that the whole notion of "unegoistic conduct," when closely examined, vanishes into air. Never yet has a man done anything solely for others and entirely without reference to a personal motive; indeed how could he possibly do anything that had no reference to himself, that is without inward compulsion (which must always have its basis in a personal need)? How could the ego act without ego?—A god, who, on the other hand, is all love, as he is usually represented, would not be capable of a solitary unegoistic act: whence one is reminded of a reflection of Lichtenberg's which is, in truth, taken from a lower sphere: "We cannot possibly feel for others, as the expression goes; we feel only for ourselves. The assertion sounds hard, but it is not, if rightly understood. A man loves neither his father nor his mother nor his wife nor his child, but simply the feelings which they inspire." Or, as La Rochefoucauld says: "If you think you love your mistress for the mere love of her, you are very much mistaken." Why acts of love are more highly prized than others, namely not on account of their nature, but on account of their utility, has already been explained in the section on the origin of moral feelings. But if a man should wish to be all love like the god aforesaid, and want to do all things for others and nothing for himself, the procedure would be fundamentally impossible because he *must* do a great deal for himself before there would be any possibility of doing anything for the love of others. It is also essential that others be sufficiently egoistic to accept always and at all times this self sacrifice and living for others, so that the men of love and self sacrifice have an interest in the survival of unloving and selfish egoists, while the highest morality, in order to maintain itself must formally enforce the existence of immorality (wherein it would be really destroying itself.)— Further: the idea of a god perturbs and discourages as long as it is accepted but as to how it originated can no longer, in the present state of comparative ethnological science, be a matter of doubt, and with the insight into the origin of this belief all faith collapses. What happens to the Christian who compares his nature with that of God is exactly what happened to Don Quixote, who depreciated his own prowess because his head was filled with the wondrous deeds of the heroes of chivalrous romance. The standard of measurement which both employ belongs to the domain of fable.—But if the idea of God collapses, so too, does the feeling of "sin" as a violation of divine rescript, as a stain upon a god-like creation. There still apparently remains that discouragement which is closely allied with fear of the punishment of worldly justice or of the contempt of one's fellow men. The keenest thorn in the sentiment of sin is dulled when it is perceived that one's acts have contravened human tradition, human rules and human laws without having thereby endangered the "eternal salvation of the soul" and its relations with deity. If finally men attain to the conviction of the absolute necessity of all acts and of their utter irresponsibility and then absorb it into their flesh and blood, every relic of conscience pangs will disappear.

134

If now, as stated, the Christian, through certain delusive feelings, is betrayed into self contempt, that is by a false and unscientific view of his acts and feelings, he must, nevertheless, perceive with the utmost amazement that this state of self contempt, of conscience pangs, of despair in particular, does not last, that there are hours during which all these things are wafted away from the soul and he feels himself once more free and courageous. The truth is that joy in his own being, the fulness of his own powers in connection with the inevitable decline of his profound excitation with the lapse of time, bore off the palm of victory. The man loves himself once more, he feels it—but this very new love, this new self esteem seems to him incredible. He can see in it only the wholly unmerited stream of the light of grace shed down upon him. If he formerly saw in every event merely warnings, threats, punishments and every kind of indication of divine anger, he now reads into his experiences the grace of god. The latter circumstance seems to him full of love, the former as a helpful pointing of the way, and his entirely joyful frame of mind now seems to him to be an absolute proof of the goodness of God. As formerly in his states of discouragement he interpreted his conduct falsely so now he does the same with his experiences. His state of consolation is now regarded as the effect produced by some external power. The love with which, at bottom, he loves himself, seems to be the divine love. That which he calls grace and the preliminary of salvation is in reality self-grace, self-salvation.

135

Therefore a certain false psychology, a certain kind of imaginativeness in the interpretation of motives and experiences is the essential preliminary to being a Christian and to experiencing the need of salvation. Upon gaining an insight into this wandering of the reason and the imagination, one ceases to be a Christian.

136
Of Christian Asceticism and Sanctity.

Much as some thinkers have exerted themselves to impart an air of the miraculous to those singular phenomena known as asceticism and sanctity, to question which or to account for which upon a rational basis would be wickedness and sacrilege, the temptation to this wickedness is none the less great. A powerful impulse of nature has in every age led to protest against such phenomena. At any rate science, inasmuch as it is the imitation of nature, permits the casting of doubts upon the inexplicable character and the supernal degree of such phenomena. It is true that heretofore science has not succeeded in its attempts at explanation. The phenomena remain unexplained still, to the great satisfaction of those who revere moral miracles. For, speaking generally, the unexplained must rank as the inexplicable, the inexplicable as the non-natural, supernatural, miraculous—so runs the demand in the souls of all the religious and all the metaphysicians (even the artists if they happen to be thinkers), whereas the scientific man sees in this demand the "evil principle."—The universal, first, apparent truth that is encountered in the contemplation of sanctity and asceticism is that their nature is complicated; for nearly always, within the physical world as well as in the moral, the apparently miraculous may be traced successfully to the complex, the obscure, the multi-conditioned. Let us venture then to isolate a few impulses in the soul of the saint and the ascetic, to consider them separately and then view them as a synthetic development.

137

There is an obstinacy against oneself, certain sublimated forms of which are included in asceticism. Certain kinds of men are under such a strong necessity of exercising their power and dominating impulses that, if other objects are lacking or if they have not succeeded with other objects they will actually tyrannize over some portions of their own nature or over sections and stages of their own personality. Thus do many thinkers bring themselves to views which are far from likely to increase or improve their fame. Many deliberately bring down the contempt of others upon themselves although they could easily have retained consideration by silence. Others contradict earlier opinions and do not shrink from the ordeal of being deemed inconsistent. On the contrary they strive for this and act like eager riders who enjoy horseback exercise most when the horse is skittish. Thus will men in dangerous paths ascend to the highest steeps in order to laugh to scorn their own fear and their own trembling limbs. Thus will the philosopher embrace the dogmas of asceticism, humility, sanctity, in the light of which his own image appears in its most hideous aspect. This crushing of self, this mockery of one's own nature, this *spernere se sperni* out of which religions have made so much is in reality but a very high development of vanity. The whole ethic of the sermon on the mount belongs in this category: man has a true delight in mastering himself through exaggerated pretensions or excessive expedients and later deifying this tyrannically exacting something within him. In every scheme of ascetic ethics, man prays to one part of himself as if it were god and hence it is necessary for him to treat the rest of himself as devil.

138
Man is Not at All Hours Equally Moral;

this is established. If one's morality be judged according to one's capacity for great, self sacrificing resolutions and abnegations (which when continual, and made a habit are known as sanctity) one is, in affection, or disposition, the most moral: while higher excitement supplies wholly new impulses which, were one calm and cool as ordinarily, one would not deem oneself even capable of. How comes this? Apparently from the propinquity of all great and lofty emotional states. If a man is brought to an extraordinary pitch of feeling he can resolve upon a fearful revenge or upon a fearful renunciation of his thirst for vengeance indifferently. He craves, under the influences of powerful emotion, the great, the powerful, the immense, and if he chances to perceive that the sacrifice of himself will afford him as much satisfaction as the sacrifice of another, or will afford him more, he will choose self sacrifice. What concerns him particularly is simply the unloading of his emotion. Hence he readily, to relieve his tension, grasps the darts of the enemy and buries them in his own breast. That in self abnegation and not in revenge the element of greatness consisted must have been brought home to mankind only after long habituation. A god who sacrifices himself would be the most powerful and most effective symbol of this sort of greatness. As the conquest of the most hardly conquered enemy, the sudden mastering of a passion—thus does such abnegation *appear*: hence it passes for the summit of morality. In reality all that is involved is the exchange of one idea for another whilst the temperament remained at a like altitude, a like tidal state. Men when coming out of the spell, or resting from such passionate excitation, no longer understand the morality of such instants, but the admiration of all who participated in the occasion sustains them. Pride is their support if the passion and the comprehension of their act weaken. Therefore, at bottom even such acts of self-abnegation are not moral inasmuch as they are not done with a strict regard for others. Rather do others afford the high strung temperament an opportunity to lighten itself through such abnegation.

139
Even the Ascetic Seeks to Make Life Easier,

and generally by means of absolute subjection to another will or to an all inclusive rule and ritual, pretty much as the Brahmin leaves absolutely nothing to his own volition but is guided in every moment of his life by some holy injunction or other. This subjection is a potent means of acquiring dominion over oneself. One is occupied, hence time does not bang heavy and there is no incitement of the personal will and of the individual passion. The deed once done there is no feeling of responsibility nor the sting of regret. One has given up one's own will once for all and this is easier than to give it up occasionally, as it is also easier wholly to renounce a desire than to yield to it in measured degree. When we consider the present relation of man to the state we perceive unconditional obedience is easier than conditional. The holy person also makes his lot easier through the complete surrender of his life personality and it is all delusion to admire such a phenomenon as the loftiest heroism of morality. It is always more difficult to assert one's personality without shrinking and without hesitation than to give it up altogether in the manner indicated, and it requires moreover more intellect and thought.

140

After having discovered in many of the less comprehensible actions mere manifestations of pleasure in emotion for its own sake, I fancy I can detect in the self contempt which characterises holy persons, and also in their acts of self torture (through hunger and scourgings, distortions and chaining of the limbs, acts of madness) simply a means whereby such natures may resist the general exhaustion of their will to live (their nerves). They employ the most painful expedients to escape if only for a time from the heaviness and weariness in which they are steeped by their great mental indolence and their subjection to a will other than their own.

141
The Most Usual Means

by which the ascetic and the sanctified individual seeks to make life more endurable comprises certain combats of an inner nature involving alternations of victory and prostration. For this purpose an enemy is necessary and he is found in the so called "inner enemy." That is, the holy individual makes use of his tendency to vanity, domineering and pride, and of his mental longings in order to contemplate his life as a sort of continuous battle and himself as a battlefield, in which good and evil spirits wage war with varying fortune. It is an established fact that the imagination is restrained through the regularity and adequacy of sexual intercourse while on the other hand abstention from or great irregularity in sexual intercourse will cause the imagination to run riot. The imaginations of many of the Christian saints were obscene to a degree; and because of the theory that sexual desires were in reality demons that raged within them, the saints did not feel wholly responsible for them. It is to this conviction that we are indebted for the highly instructive sincerity of their evidence against themselves. It was to their interest that this contest should always be kept up in some fashion because by means of this contest, as already stated, their empty lives gained distraction. In order that the contest might seem sufficiently great to inspire sympathy and admiration in the unsanctified, it was essential that sexual capacity be ever more and more damned and denounced. Indeed the danger of eternal damnation was so closely allied to this capacity that for whole generations

HUMAN, ALL TOO HUMAN

Christians showed their children with actual conscience pangs. What evil may not have been done to humanity through this! And yet here the truth is just upside down: an exceedingly unseemly attitude for the truth. Christianity, it is true, had said that every man is conceived and born in sin, and in the intolerable and excessive Christianity of Calderon this thought is again perverted and entangled into the most distorted paradox extant in the well known lines

> The greatest sin of man
> Is the sin of being born.

In all pessimistic religions the act of procreation is looked upon as evil in itself. This is far from being the general human opinion. It is not even the opinion of all pessimists. Empedocles, for example, knows nothing of anything shameful, devilish and sinful in it. He sees rather in the great field of bliss of unholiness simply a healthful and hopeful phenomenon, Aphrodite. She is to him an evidence that strife does not always rage but that some time a gentle demon is to wield the sceptre. The Christian pessimists of practice, had, as stated, a direct interest in the prevalence of an opposite belief. They needed in the loneliness and the spiritual wilderness of their lives an ever living enemy, and a universally known enemy through whose conquest they might appear to the unsanctified as utterly incomprehensible and half unnatural beings. When this enemy at last, as a result of their mode of life and their shattered health, took flight forever, they were able immediately to people their inner selves with new demons. The rise and fall of the balance of cheerfulness and despair maintained their addled brains in a totally new fluctuation of longing and peace of soul. And in that period psychology served not only to cast suspicion on everything human but to wound and scourge it, to crucify it. Man wanted to find himself as base and evil as possible. Man sought to become anxious about the state of his soul, he wished to be doubtful of his own capacity. Everything natural with which man connects the idea of badness and sinfulness (as, for instance, is still customary in regard to the erotic) injures and degrades the imagination, occasions a shamed aspect, leads man to war upon himself and makes him uncertain, distrustful of himself. Even his dreams acquire a tincture of the unclean conscience. And yet this suffering because of the natural element in certain things is wholly superfluous. It is simply the result of opinions regarding the things. It is easy to understand why men become worse than they are if they are brought to look upon the unavoidably natural as bad and later to feel it as of evil origin. It is the master stroke of religions and metaphysics that wish to make man out bad and sinful by nature, to render nature suspicious in his eyes and to so make himself evil, for he learns to feel himself evil when he cannot divest himself of nature. He gradually comes to look upon himself, after a long life lived naturally, so oppressed by a weight of sin that supernatural powers become necessary to relieve him of the burden; and with this notion comes the so called need of salvation, which is the result not of a real but of an imaginary sinfulness. Go through the separate moral expositions in the vouchers of christianity and it will always be found that the demands are excessive in order that it may be impossible for man to satisfy them. The object is not that he may become moral but that he may feel as sinful as possible. If this feeling had not been rendered agreeable to man—why should he have improvised such an ideal and clung to it so long? As in the ancient world an incalculable strength of intellect and capacity for feeling was squandered in order to increase the joy of living through feastful systems of worship, so in the era of christianity an equally incalculable quantity of intellectual capacity has been sacrificed in another endeavor: that man should in every way feel himself sinful and thereby be moved, inspired, inspirited. To move, to inspire, to inspirit at any cost—is not this the freedom cry of an exhausted, over-ripe, over cultivated age? The circle of all the natural sensations had been gone through a hundred times: the soul had grown weary. Then the saints and the ascetics found a new order of ecstacies. They set themselves before the eyes of all not alone as models for imitation to many, but as fearful and yet delightful spectacles on the boundary line between this world and the next world, where in that period everyone thought he saw at one time rays of heavenly light, at another fearful, threatening tongues of flame. The eye of the saint, directed upon the fearful significance of the shortness of earthly life, upon the imminence of the last judgment, upon eternal life hereafter; this glowering eye in an emaciated body caused men, in the old time world, to tremble to the depths of their being. To look, to look away and shudder, to feel anew the fascination of the spectacle, to yield to it, sate oneself upon it until the soul trembled with ardor and fever—that was the last pleasure left to classical antiquity when its sensibilities had been blunted by the arena and the gladiatorial show.

142
To Sum Up All That Has Been Said:

that condition of soul at which the saint or expectant saint is rejoiced is a combination of elements which we are all familiar with, except that under other influences than those of mere religious ideation they customarily arouse the censure of men in the same way that when combined with religion itself and regarded as the supreme attainment of sanctity, they are object of admiration and even of prayer—at least in more simple times. Very soon the saint turns upon himself that severity that is so closely allied to the instinct of domination at any price and which inspire even in the most solitary individual the sense of power. Soon his swollen sensitiveness of feeling breaks forth from the longing to restrain his passions within it and is transformed into a longing to master them as if they were wild steeds, the master impulse being ever that of a proud spirit; next he craves a complete cessation of all perturbing, fascinating feelings, a waking sleep, an enduring repose in the lap of a dull, animal, plant-like indolence. Next he seeks the battle and extinguishes it within himself because weariness and boredom confront him. He binds his self-deification with self-contempt. He delights in the wild tumult of his desires and the sharp pain of sin, in the very idea of being lost. He is able to play his very passions, for instance the desire to domineer, a trick so that he goes to the other extreme of abject humiliation and subjection, so that his overwrought soul is without any restraint through this antithesis. And, finally, when indulgence in visions, in talks with the dead or with divine beings overcomes him, this is really but a form of gratification that he craves, perhaps a form of gratification in which all other gratifications are blended. Novalis, one of the authorities in matters of sanctity, because of his experience and instinct, betrays the whole secret with the utmost simplicity when he says: "It is remarkable that the close connection of gratification, religion and cruelty has not long ago made men aware of their inner relationship and common tendency."

143
Not What the Saint is but what he was in

the eyes of the non-sanctified gives him his historical importance. Because there existed a delusion respecting the saint, his soul states being falsely viewed and his personality being sundered as much as possible from humanity as a something incomparable and supernatural, because of these things he attained the extraordinary with which he swayed the imaginations of whole nations and whole ages. Even he knew himself not for even he regarded his dispositions, passions and actions in accordance with a system of interpretation as artificial and exaggerated as the pneumatic interpretation of the bible. The distorted and diseased in his own nature with its blending of spiritual poverty, defective knowledge, ruined health, overwrought nerves, remained as hidden from his view as from the view of his beholders. He was neither a particularly good man nor a particularly bad man but he stood for something that was far above the human standard in wisdom and goodness. Faith in him sustained faith in the divine and miraculous, in a religious significance of all existence, in an impending day of judgment. In the last rays of the setting sun of the ancient world, which fell upon the christian peoples, the shadowy form of the saint attained enormous proportions—to such enormous proportions, indeed, that down even to our own age, which no longer believes in god, there are thinkers who believe in the saints.

144

It stands to reason that this sketch of the saint, made upon the model of the whole species, can be confronted with many opposing sketches that would create a more agreeable impression. There are certain exceptions among the species who distinguish themselves either by especial gentleness or especial humanity, and perhaps by the strength of their own personality. Others are in the highest degree fascinating because certain of their delusions shed a particular glow over their whole being, as is the case with the founder of christianity who took himself for the only begotten son of God and hence felt himself sinless; so that through his imagination—that should not be too harshly judged since the whole of antiquity swarmed with sons of god—he attained the same goal, the sense of complete sinlessness, complete irresponsibility, that can now be attained by every individual through science.—In the same manner I have viewed the saints of India who occupy an intermediate station between the christian saints and the Greek philosophers and hence are not to be regarded as a pure type. Knowledge and science—as far as they existed—and superiority to the rest of mankind by logical discipline and training of the intellectual powers were insisted upon by the Buddhists as essential to sanctity, just as they were denounced by the christian world as the indications of sinfulness.

ABOUT THE AUTHOR

Friedrich Wilhelm Nietzsche (October 15, 1844 – August 25, 1900) was a German philosopher, poet, composer, cultural critic, and classical philologist. He wrote critical texts on religion, morality, contemporary culture, philosophy, and science, displaying a fondness for metaphor, irony, and aphorism.

Nietzsche began his career as a classical philologist before turning to philosophy. In 1869, at the age of twenty-four he was appointed to the Chair of Classical Philology at the University of Basel (the youngest individual to have held this position), but resigned in the summer of 1879 due to health problems that plagued him most of his life. At the age of forty-five in 1889 he suffered a collapse and a complete loss of his mental faculties. The breakdown had been ascribed to atypical general paralysis attributed to tertiary syphilis, but this diagnosis has since come into question. He lived his remaining years in the care of his mother until her death in 1897, then under the care of his sister until his death in 1900.

His sister Elisabeth Förster-Nietzsche, acted as curator and editor of Nietzsche's manuscripts during his illness. She was married to a prominent German nationalist and anti-Semite, Bernhard Förster, and she reworked some of Nietzsche's unpublished writings to fit her husband's ideology, often in ways contrary to Nietzsche's opinions, which were strongly and explicitly opposed to anti-Semitism and nationalism (see Nietzsche's criticism of anti-Semitism and nationalism). Through Förster-Nietzsche's editions, Nietzsche's name became associated with German militarism and Nazism, but twentieth century scholars have worked hard to counteract the abuse of Nietzsche's philosophy by this ideology and rediscover the original writings of Nietzsche, unedited by his sister.

Printed in Great Britain
by Amazon.co.uk, Ltd.,
Marston Gate.